THE COMPLETE POEMS

D1334895

by the same author

ALAMEIN TO ZEM ZEM

KEITH DOUGLAS

The Complete Poems

THIRD EDITION

EDITED WITH A PREFACE BY
DESMOND GRAHAM

INTRODUCTION BY
TED HUGHES

faber and faber
LONDON·NEW YORK

First published in 1978
by Oxford University Press
second edition, with Ted Hughes's Introduction, 1987
Third edition, with revised text and new Preface, 1998
This edition published in 2000
by Faber and Faber Limited
74–77 Great Russell Street, London WC1B 3DA
Published in the United States by Faber and Faber Inc.
an affiliate of Farrar, Straus and Giroux, New York

Printed and bound in Great Britain by
TJ International Ltd, Padstow, Cornwall

A CIP record for this book
is available from the British Library

ISBN 978-0-571-27671-4

10 9 8 7 6 5

PREFACE TO THIRD EDITION

THAT a book this size should be the *Complete* poems of Keith Douglas tells a story that is both heart-rending and triumphant. It is triumphant because here are the finest British poems of the Second World War. Poems, such as *'Vergissmeinnicht'*, 'How to Kill', and 'Simplify me when I'm dead', which are now popularly anthologized, taught in schools, and widely read. Douglas was the only British poet to continue in that different war what he saw as the tradition established by Owen, Sassoon and Rosenberg. He is also a poet of the anxieties, separations, and travels of wartime; of being young in the late thirties; of the wastages of military life; and one of the best love poets of the century. His finest champion and the poet who single-handed brought about the rediscovery of Douglas's work in the early sixties, Ted Hughes, writes about these things and others in his Introduction to this book. But the story also remains, fifty-odd years after Douglas's death at twenty-four, a heart-rending story. For this collection represents what should have been the early work of an extraordinarily gifted writer. It is only Douglas's outstanding precociousness which means we have a book of this scale at all. At fourteen he was more than competent; at sixteen a master of form, with voices of his own. Before he saw action, he wrote with a seemingly effortless lucidity and command. Here then, is not a poet who was made by war but one who was killed by war. One who, through a combination of extreme talent, bloody-mindedness and sound judgement, reckoned that he would make his mark quickly because otherwise it would probably not be there at all. Douglas writes of war very much in the spirit of David Jones quoting Mandeville: '[this book] happens to be concerned with war. I should prefer it to be about a good kind of peace—but as Mandeville says, "Of Paradys ne can I not speken propurly I was not there"' (*In Parenthesis*, 1937, pp. xii–xiii). But then Douglas took this knowledge as a very good reason for not hanging about, knowing all too well he wasn't likely to get the chance to write of anything else.

Douglas's start is at Christ's Hospital—though in writing from prep. school at nine he had already proved an adept adaptor: 'When I say *I* took it up I mean I and the wing passing like running along the road with a ball while they banged and slid about us': the opposing footballers have become icebergs from Coleridge's *Ancient Mariner*. At Christ's Hospital, however, he is a star contributor to the school's literary magazine, *The Outlook*; sends poems out successfully to the main poetry magazine of the time, *New Verse*; and, preparing for later successes, publishes in *Programme* (Oxford). At Oxford for two years from October 1938, with Edmund Blunden for Tutor, he published in every available magazine; edited *The Cherwell* as a literary fortnightly; co-edited a literary miscellany *Augury* to civilize the gloom of wartime; and was included, after his departure, in the next undergraduate generation's anthology *Eight Oxford Poets*. Perhaps encouraged by the pressures of the 'Intelligences like black birds' which were coming 'on their dire wings from Europe' ('Invaders'), in the spring of his second year he gathered his poems for a collection and passed it to Blunden for comments.

Blunden, by the year's end, had sent the collection on to T. S. Eliot at Faber. Before completing his training with the old cavalry, and then armoured cars, and embarking for the Middle East in July 1941, Douglas received encouragement from Eliot but nothing more. He did send Eliot a few more poems but hearing his response to them after arriving in Egypt, he gave up attempts to publish the collection.

Douglas's first year in the Middle East was an unsatisfactory time of re-training with a tank regiment which had no serviceable tanks; getting posted to an unwanted job as camouflage expert with divisional headquarters—a job which entailed painting models of tanks and then climbing a ladder and looking down at them through the wrong end of binoculars; and moving restlessly around, meeting various girls and feeling he was simply not part of things. While he still sent poems back to his mother and to Blunden, the fate of his work in England was now in new hands.

J. C. Hall, an undergraduate acquaintance of his first year at Oxford, had published Douglas in the Oxford/Cambridge magazine *Fords and Bridges*. He had the highest opinion of his work and now wrote to Douglas's mother. He found in the poems 'a perfection which is extraordinary among poets of his generation'. He had the chance of a three-man volume and he would like to include Douglas. Mrs Douglas sent him the manuscript collection of poems which had been left with Blunden and, in October 1941, Douglas too wrote to Hall, glad at the suggestion. But by March the prospective publisher, John Lehmann, had turned down the book and Hall sent the MS back to Mrs Douglas. Then, in May, he gained a new publisher, Reginald Moore, who would include the three-man book in his Modern Reading Library series.

During this year Douglas had also made his first acquaintance with the flourishing expatriate literary world of Cairo and in July 1942 started publishing poems in a magazine there, *Citadel*. His style had been changing, continuing a move away from elaboration and ornament, which he was later to date as having started in his second year at Oxford. His work now was more metaphysical and distanced and, by September 1942, he was writing with a new political edge: about the country he lived in ('Egypt'); and, about the war-profiteer ('Christodoulos').

In October 1942, totally fed up with his jobless job, the breakdown of an engagement (to Milena in Alexandria) and the start of the El Alamein battle with him behind the lines, Douglas, famously, drove himself towards his regiment on the battlefield. He reported back to his Colonel in direct disobedience of orders, and was in action in a tank he had never seen before, the next day. All this, and his subsequent adventures as a tank commander in the desert can be read about in his now 'classic' narrative of desert warfare, *Alamein to Zem Zem*, written in 1943 and finished in London, along with illustrations he drew for it in 1944. Douglas fought through to Mersa and then, after a trip to Alexandria for supplies and new glasses, fought on with the regiment to Wadi Zem Zem. There, in January, he was wounded by triggering mines. He spent weeks in hospital at El Ballah, in Palestine, and then rejoined the regiment in May near Enfidaville, Tunisia, just as the campaign was ending. He stayed a little while in Tunisia; spent some time at Homs, Tripolitania; had leave in Palestine;

and was back in Egypt in September. By this time he had already built up a body of poems writing directly of war, explaining in a letter of 10 August 1943 to J. C. Hall (included in full at the end of this book): 'I never tried to write about war ... until I had experienced it. Now I will write of it, and perhaps one day cynic and lyric will meet and make me a balanced style.'

The idea of the war poet jotting down his poems in gaps between battlefield action is unlikely to be accurate. Douglas, in another letter (to Tambimuttu, from Homs) explained: 'What I have written has been written in hospitals, Con. depots, Base depots etc—emotion recollected in tranquillity.' A few months earlier Douglas had written an essay explaining why the war had not yet (1943) produced any poet of note: 'there is nothing new, from a soldier's point of view, about this war except its mobile character ... almost all that a modern poet on active service is inspired to write, would be tautological ... it seems to me that the whole body of English war poetry of this war, civil and military, will be created after the war is over.'

By July 1943 Douglas's fortunes as a poet had, potentially, dramatically changed. Hall's support had led, after publisher's delays, to the publication of *Selected Poems* that February, though Douglas did not receive notice of this till May. He had had time to recover and convalesce as the result of his wounds, time to write. Now, out of the blue, he received a letter from M. J. Tambimuttu. Tambimuttu (known as Tambi) edited the main London poetry magazine of the war, *Poetry (London)*, and with it, was editor for Nicholson and Watson's poetry imprint, 'Editions Poetry London'. He had come across two poems by Douglas in the May 1939 issue of *Fords and Bridges*. So impressed was he, he sought out Mrs Douglas's address and wrote asking her permission to reprint the poems, to send on any work she had from Douglas, and to let him have his address. At the end of May, Douglas received a letter from Tambi, inviting him to send poems. By 11 July he had a letter offering him publication of a book-length selection. The importance of this encouragement, and of John Hall's support, cannot be over-estimated. Taking up Tambi's offer Douglas wrote: 'Thank you for your letter and for publishing my poems—I had given up all idea of writing in the Army until your efforts and John Hall's nerved me to try again.' When Douglas left the Middle East in November he had completed his narrative as far as his Zem Zem wound and had most of the war poems on which his reputation now rests. Some of these poems he left for publication with *Personal Landscape* which had recently started to publish him.

Douglas had no wish to go back to England and what was sure to be more fighting as mainland Europe was assaulted. At one time there appeared possibilities for him to stay in Egypt but once his regiment prepared to leave, he felt his place was with them. Back in Britain in December 1943, he had some weeks leave in Oxford, 'before being fattened up for the slaughter', working on his manuscripts and on the narrative and making illustrations. He visited London and Tambimuttu and, at the publisher's offices, met Tambi's assistant Betty Jesse, with whom he started a close and complicated friendship which blossomed into a sort of love affair. Meanwhile 'the stomach of a war' ('Actors waiting') rumbled ominously. Douglas took final leave, first official and then unofficial: to see Betty—to the fury of at least one comrade, who felt that his leaving their sealed camp endangered the whole invasion of Europe. By April he had left with Betty and Tambi all the poems he could manage. On 4 April he sent back a last, beautifully written manuscript on top quality paper: the poem 'On a Return from Egypt'.

Damned throughout his life to bad circumstances, losses and changes brought on him by others, Douglas had a genius for making the most of the occasion: a genius which had earlier produced his own epitaph on leaving England for military service abroad, 'Simplify me when I'm dead'. Now it produced first, the valedictory poem 'Women of four countries': ('Here I give back perforce / the sweet wine to the grape'), and then 'On a Return from Egypt', his definition of the place to which his struggles and achievements had been brought: 'And all my endeavours are unlucky explorers / come back, abandoning the expedition; / . . . but time, time is all I lacked / to find them, as the great collectors before me.'

Douglas had achieved much in his work on his collection. Poems, presumably only in draft before, such as 'Mersa', 'Egyptian Sentry' and 'L'Autobus' were only completed now and by April he had left about one hundred poems with the publisher. He had not completed the Preface he wanted to write but he had left a title *Bête Noire*, a jacket design and a note to accompany it. Although he had consistently said that the poems would need to be arranged in sections to mark the stages of his work, he left no final record as to the grouping he wanted.

When Douglas was killed in Normandy on 9 June 1944 there were few obituaries. *Poetry (London)* had not appeared for eighteen months, though when, in December *Poetry (London)* No. X did appear, it included a fine obituary by Tambimuttu and a number of Douglas's poems. Then *Poetry (London)* and Editions Poetry London went quiet for some time. In 1946 *Alamein to Zem Zem* was published, with an appendix of sixteen poems, mainly from the war. *Bête Noire*, still advertised, was never to appear. Tambimuttu had vanished from London by 1948 and the publishing house was on the way to bankruptcy. A new owner, Richard March, set about rescuing Douglas's work as virtually the publishing house's final effort. He sorted and copied the MSS Douglas had left; sought advice from John Waller; and then, with Waller and G. S. Fraser as editors, published *Collected Poems* in 1951.

My first edition of *The Complete Poems* in 1978 brought in all the evidence gained from my work on Douglas's biography: adding new poems, a more accurate chronology, and printing the latest text for each poem. The differences between that edition and its predecessors are spelt out in my Preface to that edition. Since then, a second edition with Ted Hughes' Introduction appeared in 1987, and was reissued in 1995. Still no significant textual changes were made. Now, twenty years on, this third edition retains the contents and presentation (with all sources, important variants and textual notes at the back), and chronology of the first. The texts of seven poems, however, have been significantly altered and another dozen have received minor changes. To my relief, fewer than a handful of these changes result from corrections (an 'on' for 'in' in 'The Knife'; a hyphen here, a couple of commas there). I have taken the liberty of regularizing the rhymes in 'Canoe'—'part of / art of'—where previously I printed the lines as did *The Cherwell* under Douglas's editorship. Checking over ambiguous autograph revisions to 'I listen to the desert wind', I have deleted 'cold' from line 10 as metrically irregular.

The significant changes arise from a slightly different approach to the same policy as I had employed previously: a policy of printing the latest available text for each poem. I now wish to give more status to the idea of the collection Douglas was himself preparing in 1944. In the case of poems he wrote before leaving for the Middle East he delivered to the publisher a batch of folio typescripts, with a title page and address. Some of these carried autograph revisions, most none. It is texts from these typescripts which I have now printed in the case of seven poems, although later texts do exist. 'Love and Gorizia' becomes 'Bexhill', '.303' and 'Strange Gardener' are altered, as are 'The Garden' (now 'Absence') and 'A Speech for An Actor' (now 'Leukothea'), 'A Ballet', and 'John Anderson'. I have used the published version of 'Youth' on the grounds that Douglas had copies of *Outlook* to hand in 1944, and I have had a new look at the autograph revisions to 'The Creator'.

Second, I have in two crucial cases introduced a new element into my discrimination between different copies made by Douglas. Experience with publishing my own poems has taught me that versions sent to an editor with a view to publication have a different status for the poet from versions sent to others, even if eventual publication of them is not out of the question. So, I have printed here the version of 'Behaviour of Fish' which Douglas sent to Tambimuttu (and which coincides with the version he left for publication with *Personal Landscape*). Finally, and to my delight, I have been able to print 'Aristocrats' rather than 'Sportsmen' in the body of the text. 'Aristocrats' Douglas sent to Tambimuttu, hoping he would publish the poem. 'Sportsmen' (now printed in the Notes) remains, as far as I can ascertain, the later version; however, the paper of the autograph MS is folded so as to fit an envelope, suggesting it was not a copy made and held by Douglas but one sent in a letter. Another poem exists in a similar MS, a version of '*Vergissmeinnicht*' called 'The Lover'. The recipient was most probably Mrs Douglas, though it could have been a girl-friend, Olga Meiersens, who subsequently returned Douglas's letters to his mother. That Douglas intended Tambi to publish the versions sent as 'Aristocrats' is left in no doubt by his sending the poem in two forms—airgraph and letter—and copying in capitals those words which might have been difficult to read.

My full acknowledgements are listed in the first edition. Here I must thank Jacqueline Simms, formerly of Oxford University Press; Christopher Fletcher of the British Library MS Dept.; and, above all, Trude Schwab. I would also like to re-emphasise my thanks to John Hall, who has been a great help to me and a splendid Trustee of Douglas's estate for many years. Finally, and again, my deepest gratitude must go to Catharine Carver, who died in 1991. She showed me the way with everything I have written on Douglas, and much more.

All the biographical material here is taken from my *Keith Douglas 1920–1944: A Biography* (OUP 1974; 1988). Quotations from letters relating to publication are taken from my *Keith Douglas: A Prose Miscellany* (Carcanet 1985).

DESMOND GRAHAM

Newcastle upon Tyne
May 1999

CONTENTS

ARMY: ENGLAND

ARMY: MIDDLE EAST

ENGLAND 1944

INTRODUCTION

1

KEITH DOUGLAS was born on 24 January 1920, in Tunbridge
Wells, and was killed in action on 9 June 1944, near the village
of St Pierre, three days after the first Normandy invasion.

A taste for his poetry has been slow to develop. The critical
odds against any immediate post-war recognition were quite
weighty. The *Four Quartets*, published the year Douglas died,
joined the continuing prime of Auden's generation, the emergence
of Dylan Thomas's generation, and the rapid maturing of the
survivors of the 1920 generation. On top of these, the same years
had to make room for the arrival, in the fifties, of virtually the
whole range of modern US poetry (together with its New Criti-
cism); followed during the late fifties and early sixties by the Beats
(together with the astounding surge of island collaboration that
rose to welcome them); followed, from the mid-sixties onwards,
by the modern poetry of the entire surrounding world, in that
unprecedented boom of translation.

Through those same years, when the world was being so viol-
ently rearranged under the multiple irradiations of the nuclear
bomb, poetry had entered a new era of evolutionary tests. And
the explosion of poetic mutants (outflanking the dictum: 'No more
poetry after Auschwitz'), promoting themselves in every niche,
each hoping to have hit on the right adaptation for survival, is
obviously still going on.

All these factors are relevant to the tardiness of the growth of
Douglas's reputation, and to what makes him so interesting now,
four decades after his death. Looking back, it is no wonder if his
few pages were mislaid for a while. The *Collected Poems*, published
in 1951 by Editions Poetry London Ltd, with notes by his friends
John Waller and G. S. Fraser, sank immediately out of circulation
and was not reprinted.

But he didn't disappear completely. And his slow steps back
to the living tell a persuasive story.

One or two poems kept turning up in anthologies. Then in the late fifties a quite large batch was selected by the US Editors Hall, Pack and Simpson for their anthology, *New Poets of England And America* (counterblast to this, *The New American Poetry*, was the anthology that woke up the US literary world to the full deployment of the Beats). This group of Douglas's poems amounted to a modest revival for him, and he began to find some new readers among the post-war generation. But it was a slow business. When his mother asked for his *Collected Poems* in a Kent bookshop as late as 1962, all six copies of the 1951 order were still on the shelf.

Nevertheless, his return had begun. Faber & Faber published a selection in 1964, and then in 1966 a new *Collected Poems*, with updated notes by the original editors and J. C. Hall, and a new introduction by Edmund Blunden, who had been Douglas's tutor at Oxford (and had from the start recognized his gift). Seven years later Oxford University Press published the excellent biography of Douglas by Desmond Graham, and in 1978 a new *Complete Poems*, edited by Graham, with detailed textual notes and extensive changes within the text itself. But a more suggestive indication of just how far Douglas had emerged into the consciousness of poets and poetry readers was revealed by chance in an odd way. In 1984 the Poetry Society held a poll, and he appeared among the top ten poets most favoured by members of the Society.

This light-hearted election might not mean a great deal for the other nine, but it must be significant for a poet who had died forty years before, on the far side of that post-war cataclysm of poetic and psychological revolutions, and who left only a handful of short poems, nearly all of them written before he was twenty-four. It is also significant that his reputation had matured up to this point so slowly, through a seasoning of such extremes. There is nothing of the brittle éclat of a 'rediscovery' about it. His evident solidity has been unveiled by a very gradual and quite well-observed lifting of the mists. Very much, in fact, as Wilfred Owen's achievement asserted itself.

2

Douglas is one of those in whom the man and the poet are close. There seems not much apparatus—symbolic or intellectual system, or even descriptive intent—between his urgent, conflicted, highly assertive nature, and the naked physique of the poetry. The poems tend to disappear into one's idea of him. Their relationship to him is like that of a speech in a play to the character who speaks it, rather than to the dramatist. They are less an 'opus', less a created world, than simply a few examples of his extraordinary way of doing things. The visually definite settings of some of the best poems—'*Vergissmeinnicht*', 'How to Kill', 'Cairo Jag'—are little more than arenas where his poetry tests and defines its code of behaviour, or, rather where he tests and defines himself. In this way each poem is a spiritual or rather psychic exercise, a moral exercise.

The incisive nimble glance, the uniquely tempered music, the simple, point-blank, bull's-eye statement, the tensile delicacy, are all part of Douglas' effort to confront reality undeluded, and as it were on its own terms, and yet maintain detachment and self-control. Each line gives a strong impression of acrobatic balance involving the whole body: a feat of graceful, outer physical balance improvised over a pit of turbulent, inner, psychic unbalance. This balancing act in words, which draws the reader into the same imperilled concentration as Douglas's own, achieves, at its best, convincing authority, distinction, beauty, finality, and even, one feels, practical utility. But it is precariously brought off: each step on the high wire is somehow acutely suspenseful, a dramatic hazard, as the foot lifts up over something difficult to face (which is nevertheless being faced).

He was interested in certain rules of military discipline, leftovers of the old heroic code, but with quite personal refinements, or fanaticisms, blended in. What he makes of it is pervaded by his aesthetic preoccupation with a slightly zen-like martial art of 'grace': beauty as perfect simplicity, beauty as perfect reality, beauty as perfect integrity, beauty as perfect action. In Mishima's aestheticised Samurai credo, *Sun and Steel*, one catches unexpected reflections of Douglas.

These exercises are also dance games. That physical presence of the whole person, in musical sequences and patterns of such vivacity and variety of cadence and pace, suggests that idea of a dancer, sometimes a marionette. The peculiar aura of masked or dead-pan pathos which clings to his gestures and inflections, to the startling leaps and abrupt stillness, reminds one of the pathos of puppets—those puppets, maybe, which do appear frequently in the poems, prancing across the flimsy scenery, with their painted faces, in their paper costumes, or lying discarded. This hieratic, marionette quality is an apt dramatis personae for the passionate, fatalistic outlook which is the gimbal control of Douglas's balancing act, where the nonchalance is also, as on a puppet's face, anguish, the bravura a harrowing posture of doll's hands, the gallantry a cool acceptance of the worst possible fate. The source of the stage-lighting of this whole performance is, perhaps, that thing difficult to face—a vision of his own early death, his own death already foresuffered.

3

With such a dark horse as Douglas, the pedigree becomes interesting. French and German (Castellain and Huth, brokers and bankers) on his mother's side, and, on his father's, Scots and Scots-Canadian. As an only child, his main companion through early childhood was his French grandfather. Soon after his father's return home from military service in 1922, young Douglas switched allegiance and adopted military dress: with metal buttons, puttees, and a medal made out of a halfpenny, he patrolled the garden, challenging all who passed. His infatuation with this colourful, ebullient father, so suddenly returned from the wars, seems to have been intense and from that time his obsession for playing soldiers came near to dominating his life.

Domestic accidents followed which, one imagines, encouraged him to rationalize his emotional investments, reducing them, perhaps, if possible, to something that would fit into a kit-bag. When

Douglas was four, his mother collapsed with encephalitis. This illness dragged on (and recurred throughout Douglas's adolescence), the family smallholding business failed, and on borrowed money Keith was sent, at the age of six, to a boarding school. Two years later, his father moved away to North Wales and it soon became clear that he had gone for good. So, at the age of eight, Keith became in a way responsible for his mother.

The masters at his first school found him difficult: 'bumptious and aggressive', too bitingly critical, too unorthodox, too fond of his own fantastic methods, too clever for his own good. His next school, Christ's Hospital, only managed to contain him by being exceptionally forgiving and flexible. His biography helps us to understand this. His whole childhood can be seen both as a nursery for his peculiar alienation, or what he called his 'long pain', and as a forcing house for the unusual strain of independence in his character. He pondered this a good deal, partly because he could see how much dislike it provoked. From quite an early age, he showed an acute awareness of somehow having to manage inside himself some extra thing that was almost unmanageable.

After two years at Oxford, where he edited *Cherwell* and led a visible career as poet and personality, he entered the Army in 1940, went through training as a Cavalry Officer, and eventually arrived on the North African desert as a Tank Commander with the Sherwood Rangers. The eventful story of his war there is told in his memoir *Alamein to Zem Zem*, but the inner drama, which is more germane to the poems, shaped itself around the conflict between one or two tortuous love affairs and the claims of Army life. Desmond Graham's sensitive account of these relationships, as of the earlier ones at Oxford, reveals the curiously despairing nature of Douglas's search for emotional anchorage, his loneliness, the frailty of his equilibrium, and his fatalism. Reading of these episodes in his biography, one begins almost to fear for him. There seems to be something tenuous, even provisional, in his attachment to life: in spite of his energetic appetite for it, and the pains he took to make its special moments delightful, he seems to have been ready, at any moment, to leave it. He displays, in lofty measure, heroic disregard for it. But something more too.

Throughout his letters, and in the remarks remembered by his friends, as in his poems, recurs the cool note of certainty that he will soon be killed. It is impossible to say which exercises most sway: the premonition of this death in action, or the sealed hopelessness of his 'long pain'. Some sort of inner betrothal between the two has taken place, and all his efforts at outer engagement seem forsworn. The portrait of this disquieting union hovers like a double exposure behind the brightly lit foreground of almost every poem. In a sense it was his subject. All the later poems seem preoccupied by it. In each one he simultaneously confronts and disarms it, sometimes only by catching the visionary moment in his bare hand:

> ... only his silken
> intentions severed with a single splinter.

Or, even closer:

> The weightless mosquito touches
> her tiny shadow on the stone,
> and with how like, how infinite
> a lightness, man and shadow meet.
> They fuse. A shadow is a man
> when the mosquito death approaches.

Until finally, in his last lines:

> The next month, then, is a window
> and with a crash I'll split the glass.
> Behind it stands one I must kiss,
> person of love or death,
> a person or a wraith,
> I fear what I shall find.

On the morning 9 June 1944, when a mortar fragmentation bomb exploded in a tree above him, he was killed by a splinter so fine that no wound showed on his body.

4

As a 'war poet' he seems fitted to his war, just as Owen seems fitted to his. The relationship between the two poets is intriguing. To a degree, the overall shaping psychological influence on the Second World War was knowledge of the fearful lessons of the First, the punished, mobilized experience remembering the helpless, immobilized innocence. Even the distinctive and decisive new physical factor of the Second—mechanized mobility—was like a materialization of the will to correct the costliest disadvantage of the First. In a similar way Douglas's poetic strategies can be seen as a reverse image of Owen's. One can detect between the two a certain system of correspondences, polarized across what both saw to be the crucial battle experience of killing and being killed.

In Owen, this experience became all but an actualization of Christ's suffering and death. Through it, he was able to reach that depth and inclusiveness of compassionate feeling which makes us think of him as a 'major' poet, a poet who transcended his personal limitations and spoke for a people. In Douglas the same act, of killing and being killed, becomes something quite different. It becomes the touchstone epiphany of the cruelty—or indifference—of a purely material Creation in which man is one of the working parts, where Life, for all its desirability, is ultimately futile and the living are hardly more than deluded variants of the dead. Instead of a religious depth of compassion uniting him to all men, what Douglas attains is a flexible, existential temper of outlook which enables him to confront annihilation and meaninglessness, and still feel life is worth the effort. In a meaningless Universe, on the brink of annihilation, it may be a useful temper to have perfected, but it does not lessen his loneliness, rather intensifies it, and in the end he speaks for no one but himself.

Aspects of this opposite polarization between the two poets are typical of much else about them. It even appears in their attitudes to their mothers, in Owen's case abnormally, even amazingly, enamoured; responsible for, and preoccupied with, but detached and independent, in the case of Douglas. This is an image, also, of their attitudes to feeling, and of their respective relationships, as it happened, to the physical circumstances of the actual fighting.

Some of the changes that had evolved between Owen and Douglas show up clearly in a comparison of Owen's 'Last Laugh' with Douglas's 'Gallantry'. Between Owen's:

> Another sighed,—'O Mother, mother! Dad!'
> Then smiled, at nothing, childlike, being dead.
>> And the lofty Shrapnel-cloud
>> Leisurely gestured,—Fool!
>> And the falling splinters tittered.
>
> 'My Love!' one moaned. Love-languid seemed his mood,
> Till, slowly lowered his whole face kissed the mud.
>> And the Bayonets' long teeth grinned;
>> Rabbles of Shells hooted and groaned;
>> And the Gas hissed.

And Douglas's:

> Conrad luckily survived the winter:
> he wrote a letter to welcome
> the auspicious spring: only his silken
> intentions severed with a single splinter.
>
> Was George fond of little boys?
> We always suspected it,
> but who will say: since George was hit
> we never mention our surmise.
>
> It was a brave thing the Colonel said,
> but the whole sky turned too hot
> and the three heroes never heard what
> it was, gone deaf with steel and lead.
>
> But the bullets cried with laughter,
> the shells were overcome with mirth,
> plunging their heads in steel and earth—
> (the air commented in a whisper).

In Owen's poem it is the conceit of amusement which does the damage. In Douglas, however, the same idea becomes the precise focus for an ironic and savage aptness which all but redeems the poem. We feel Owen is taking a juvenile holiday, in those shorter lines, from his mature, sacred solidarity with the wounded and killed, which are his real reserves; whereas Douglas is drawing on his only reserves and they are—the internal-combustion engine, then animal pragmatism, then nothing. The human world is smaller in Douglas, but deconsecrated in every direction more limited and the limits more clearly defined, but it is perhaps now more familiar.

'*Vergissmeinnicht*' is as final and universal an image of one of the ultimate battle experiences as exists on any page. Yet it could have been written by some visiting war correspondent during a weekend revolutionary coup. Or on any front from the last war up to the present moment. In other words, it is as sharply characteristic of modern attitudes to battle as it is of Douglas. The same can be said of 'How to Kill'. This poem is quite perfect in its way, yet it evokes no sense of actual battle, of nightmare, enclosing conflict, of inescapable, immovable war, such as breathes from the least fragment of Owen's. It is impossible to imagine it being written in the earlier war, by someone known to Sassoon or Graves, or to Trakl or Rilke. Yet it could have been written on any front, in any skirmish, since Douglas wrote it, and even written by somebody not a soldier at all, perhaps by a terrorist, or some mountain bandit, far from any war or political quarrel, one of those characters of supreme, heartless professionalism but supreme 'essence', such as Gourdjieff describes, gazing a whole day over the sights of a rifle, waiting for the traveller. What is distinctive about it is just that 'essence', that individualized temper superior to all circumstances, the diamond quality that has already survived the ultimate ordeals, a salamander quality that can act, and can remain intact and effective—and even feel at home—in the fires of the end.

Most significantly for the poems, that polar opposition of Owen and Douglas can be found clearest of all in the music of the lines. A good deal has been said about the dominant feminine component in the timbre of Owen's lines: the savouring clasp and caress of the syllables, which operate almost methodically, like separate palps of the clinging senses; the slow, mesmerized procedure; the pervasive, passive eroticism of wounds and death; the luxurious almost rapturous love-death love-act atmosphere about even the most horrific realizations, or rather especially about those; the solemn chords and crescendos of holy consummation, more often Wagner than Elgar.

Everything about Douglas's verbal patterning eschews that music. The dominant component of Douglas's line suggests a masculine movement, a nimble, predatory attack, hard-edged, with a quick and clean escape. It rides through the vocal inflection of the whole sentence like the masterfully steered swerve of a bird:

> incendiary in tint, so swift he
> searches about the sky for room,
>
> towering like the cliffs of this coast
> with his stiletto wing
> and orange on his breast:
>
> he has consumed and drained
> the colours of the sea
> and the yellow of this tidal ground
>
> till he escapes the eye, or is a ghost
> and in a moment has come down
> crept into the dead bird, ceased to exist.

One has the impression, too, that inside each line an entirely fresh melody starts up, forges a quick path against our expectation, and leaves the line as a trace of its passage, while a quite different melody, from some unexpected angle, inscribes another flourish beneath it, followed by another just as surprising. Equally remarkable is the natural ease with which these spontaneous-seeming cadences form the larger musical structures of stanza and whole poem. This sense of endless melodic invention and architectural variety is one of the delights of Douglas, the strongest characteristic even in

> Ono-no-komache the poetess
> sat on the ground among her flowers,
> sat in her delicate-patterned dress
> thinking of the rowers,
> thinking of the god Daikoku.

and throughout that flawless poem of his sixteenth year.

Within Owen's ground bass his empathy with the wounded and killed suggests a supine figure, submissive to the fullness of the experience. Within Douglas's music there moves something suggestive of the solitary protagonist of a danced drama, not the compassionate one but the afflicted, agile in his dance, irrepressible but in pain, a Marsyas half-flayed, a satyr with a piercing flute. The music is familiar and intimate, like the inner voice of one's own voice, yet a desolate sort of music, closer to the crying of a bird than to the massed organ tones of great abbeys audible in Owen.

> As the processes of earth
> strip off the colour and the skin
> take the brown hair and the blue eye
>
> and leave me simpler than at birth
> when hairless I came howling in
> as the moon came in the cold sky.

This clean lightness of Douglas is inscribed on a gem, and irreducible. Much of Owen's strength is brought to bear by his measured, polyphonic beat and saturated weight. But Douglas's extempore-seeming, lightly percussive, soloist, syncopated unpredictability, like the graph of the brain's electrical responses, is paradoxically strong. In his poem 'Words' he describes the airy lightness of his method:

> . . . There are those who capture them
> in hundreds, keep them prisoners in black
> bottles, release them at exercise and clap them back.
> But I keep words only a breath of time
> turning in the lightest of cages—uncover
> and let them go: sometimes they escape for ever.

Yet the effect is of a fine-spun, intricate steeliness, like the structure of a flying insect, all cantilever tension and balance, a flexing of minute precisions, iridescent but definite, and at the same time like the skeleton of a small, transparent, deep-sea fish that withstands giant pressures.

Douglas arrived at this fusion of elemental substantiality and lightness with hard labour. In Graham's biography a series of drafts of the second verse of 'How to Kill' show what unremarkable prosody he groped through towards the final crystalline design, and, in the last stage, what very slight adjustments of angle and stress brought the whole instrument suddenly to life, perfectly tuned to the Douglas music, which is also (as if this were the conclusive law) a natural, undistorted pattern of expressive speech.

A less complete but perhaps more striking example of the same process occurs between the final version of '*Vergissmeinnicht*' and the early draft printed in Keith Douglas's *Prose Miscellany* (Carcanet), which runs as follows:

A DEAD GUNNER

> Three weeks since pierced by flung metal
> the sound steel broke beside my belly
> (drew us back shattered): the turret in a flurry
> of blood and Bilby quite still, dribbling spittle,
>
> and we advanced and knocked out that gun
> and the crew got away somehow
> to skulk in the mountains until now
> the campaign over. (But) they left one,

they left you, perhaps the boy
to whom Steffy had written Vergissmeinnicht
on this photograph in the ditch. Perhaps the hand
that gave Evans and Bilby their last gift

For we see you with a sort of content
Abased, seeming to have paid
mocked by your own durable equipment
the metal beneath your decaying head undecayed

Yet she would weep to see how you are fallen away
and on your back the great blowflies move
and the dust gathering in your paper eye
your stomach open in a stinking cave.

yes here the lover and the killer lie mingled
for the two have but one body and one heart
and death that had the cruel soldier singled
out, has done the lover mortal hurt.

To compare with this rough block the poem Douglas extricated
from it is to observe in action what he knew about economy and
penetration, compact simplicity and the electrodes of montage,
the path of the nerve under language, tensile strength.

Tracking him from his origins through his arduous upbringing
and all the accidents of his unusual temperament, one can under-
stand that the balance of pressures, out of which he drew his
style, might well have produced something unique—uniquely
constituted, uniquely tested, a triumph peculiar to that man in
that place at that time. In fact he ended up close to the poetry of
a very different individual:

> The still explosions on the rocks,
> the lichens, grow
> by spreading, gray, concentric shocks.
> They have arranged
> to meet the rings around the moon, although
> within our memories they have not changed.

Elizabeth Bishop and Keith Douglas share enough of the same

precise light, the same restless, intimately subjective accompaniment to a severely objective outlook, the same intimate immediacy of vocal inflection and naked truth of tone, to make either of them remind us of the other (and really of nobody else). Curiously enough, they also share that inclination to a hieratic, marionettish, inner detachment and pitching of the voice, which may have to do with similarities in a passionate but stylized alienation, or may simply be a common sensitivity to the puppet-quality of spirit-life—which is also common to so much primitive, or ritual, drama and to Noh. The two poets seem closest of all in their sleight of snakes-and-ladders interconnections and collisions between disparate levels of experience and mood, a naturally rambling, wittily playful, magpie reportage which touches, at each point, the resonance of a controlling music and a quite other vision of the same subject—related again, maybe, to that inner ritual stage:

> Marcelle drops her Gallic airs and tragedy
> suddenly shrieks in Arabic about the fare
> with the cabman, links herself so
> with the somnambulists and legless beggars:
> it is all one, all as you have heard.

> But by a day's travelling you reach a new world
> the vegetation is of iron
> dead tanks, gun barrels split like celery
> the metal brambles have no flowers or berries
> and there are all sorts of manure, you can imagine
> the dead themselves, their boots, clothes and possessions
> clinging to the ground, a man with no head
> has a packet of chocolate and a souvenir of Tripoli.

Had Douglas read:

> this cartoon by Raphael for a tapestry for a Pope;
> it does look like heaven.
> But a skeletal lighthouse standing there
> in black and white clerical dress,
> who lives on his nerves, thinks he knows better,

He thinks that hell rages below his feet,
that is why the shallow water is so warm . . .

of 'Florida' or 'The Monument' that Elizabeth Bishop later pub-
lished in her first book in 1946?

Comparing the two, it is surprising to find that, in spite of all
the tantalizing echoes, the variety and accent of her music is
neither so rich nor so compelling as his, and that she knew nothing
of that overdrive moment in Douglas, that effect of sudden fore-
shortening, the abrupt impatient short-cut where his seriousness
opens and he arrives at the core of his inspiration:

. . . Each time the night discards

draperies on the eyes and leaves the mind awake
I look each side of the door of sleep
for the little coin it will take
to buy the secret I shall not keep.

Her pictures are no doubt larger, more complicated, with qualities
of charm and subtlety and perspective quite outside Douglas's
register, and in the comparison he can seem raw, battlegrimed,
rough and ready. Even so, one returns to him, from such a master
as Elizabeth Bishop, with even keener respect.

One other link with Owen brings this present collection directly
to the reader. Owen carried about, in his pocket, photographs of
trench horrors which he would evidently have liked to see magni-
fied and put on public display in London, his idea being to shock
his non-participant fellow citizens into an awareness of the new
day dawning in the trenches. One can't help wondering how
much of this passionately formulated but frustrated motive
diverted itself into the graphic focus and massive, direct appeal
of his poetry. When he declared 'The Poetry Does Not Matter'
what he also meant was that in the poems nothing mattered
but truth to the facts, the deepest possible grasp of the human
implications of the facts, and expressiveness—irresistible com-
munication on the most private, the most affecting level. The
poetic style which he bred out of Sassoon on one side and the
dramatic verse of Yeats on the other was a means to this end,

and the qualities for which we admire it, the basic simplicity, the shocking directness, the colloquial flexibility, the musical, sensuous allure and warmth of its embrace, the calm, open confrontation, were almost by-products, and incidental; they grew out of, or were commissioned or commandeered by, that purpose. After perfecting this means, and producing a few examples of what could be done with it, Owen died and bequeathed it to others. (The standard model, as in such a poem as 'Smile, Smile, Smile', was duly taken over, with only a few modifications, by, for instance, Philip Larkin.)

In his different way, Douglas did something similar. As with Owen, all the accidents of his life had prepared in him what the war required in its poetic spokesman, and what the war helped him to turn, briefly, to full poetic account. Writing to J. C. Hall in 1943 he said: 'But my object (and I don't give a damn about my duty as a poet) is to write true things, significant things, in words each of which works for its place in the line.' He is more explicit: 'I don't know if you have come across the word Bullshit—it is an Army word and signifies humbug and unnecessary detail. It symbolises what I think must be got rid of—the mass of irrelevancies, of "attitudes", "approaches", propaganda, ivory towers, etc., that stands between us and our problems and what we have to do about them.' He deliberately applied himself to a style of reportage and documentary, with the conscious idea, as can be seen here, of some kind of service to the tribe, of a common task to be undertaken selflessly. He practised this style throughout *Alamein to Zem Zem*, but it culminated in the sharp, hard focus of the last few poems. After hectoring Hall about the realistic, minimal hopes and maximum efforts vital to the times, he goes on: '. . . all this may make it easier for you to understand why I am writing the way I am and why I shall never go back to the old forms. You may even begin to see some virtue in it. To be sentimental or emotional now is dangerous to oneself and to others. To trust anyone or to admit any hope of a better world is criminally foolish, as foolish as it is to stop working for it. It sounds silly to say to work without hope, but it can be done; it's only a form of insurance; it doesn't mean work hopelessly.'

This purposeful, high, official motive was in a sense the rationale and authorization of the outlook he had been wrestling towards all his life, but under the new pressure of it he perfected his style as if incidentally, almost as a by-product, an essential utility for the job in hand, rather as Owen did. Like Owen's, though so different from his, it is a general, all-purpose style, stripped to the functional minimum, open to experience and exploratory, a kit for emergency use under adverse, extreme circumstances, yet capable of the intensity, grace and music of a high art. And like Owen, after producing a few examples of what could be done with it, he died and left it to others.

TED HUGHES
[1987]

KEITH DOUGLAS 1920–1944

A Chronology

1920	24 Jan.	Keith Castellain Douglas born at Tunbridge Wells
1920–6		At Cranleigh, Surrey
1926–31		Boarder at Edgeborough School, Guildford
1928		KD's father, Capt. Keith Sholto Douglas, leaves family; KD does not see him again
1931–8		At school at Christ's Hospital, Horsham
1935		Holiday at Gorizia in northern Italy
1936		Makes first collection of poems
1938	March	Published in *New Verse*
1938–40		At Merton College, Oxford, reading English with Edmund Blunden as tutor
1939	September	War declared. KD enlists at once; call-up deferred, returns to Oxford
1940	April	Editor of *The Cherwell*, publishing many poems there and in other Oxford periodicals. Makes second collection of poems
	May	Co-editor of *Augury*, a literary miscellany
	July	Joins up as cavalry trooper, Redford Barracks. Leaves collection with Blunden in hope of publication
	Sept.–Oct.	Training at Army Equitation School, Weedon
	Nov.–Jan. 1941	Officer Cadet at Sandhurst
1941	February	Commissioned into Second Derbyshire Yeomanry at Ripon. T. S. Eliot praises collection passed to him by Blunden, but does not offer publication
	March–June	With regiment at Wickwar, Glos.
	May	Gunnery Course at Linney Head. Sends four more poems to Eliot
	June	Sails for Middle East. Leaves collection with mother
	August	Arrives in Egypt

	October	At Nathanya, Palestine, convalescing after ear infection. J. C. Hall proposes publication of KD's poems in a shared selection
	28 Oct.	Joins cavalry regiment, the Sherwood Rangers Yeomanry, in Palestine
	November	Visits Syria
1942	February	Posted to Division H.Q. in Palestine as Camouflage Staff Officer
	May–June	In Cairo; spends time with David Hicks, editor of *Citadel*, and meets Bernard Spencer
	July–Sept.	In Alexandria
	October	At Wadi Natrun, to be with H.Q. in forthcoming offensive. First poems in *Poetry (London)*
	23 Oct.	Battle of El Alamein begins
	27 Oct.	KD defies orders and leaves H.Q. to report to his regiment at El Alamein; in battle next day
	9 Nov.	At Mersa
	23 Nov.	Leaves Mersa and rejoins advance towards Tripoli
1943	15 Jan.	Wounded in action at Wadi Zem Zem
	25 Jan.	Arrives at No. 1 General Hospital, El Ballah, Palestine. In six weeks there writes first group of war poems and probably begins his narrative of the desert fighting (*Alamein to Zem Zem*)
	February	*Selected Poems*, by KD, J. C. Hall, and Norman Nicholson, published
	April	On leave in Tel Aviv and Alexandria
	6 May	Rejoins regiment outside Enfidaville; no further part in fighting; campaign ends eight days later
	May–June	In Tunisia, regiment resting; made captain. Writes second group of war poems
	11 July	At Homs, Tripolitania, agrees to prepare a selection of poems for Editions Poetry London
	Sept.–Nov.	In Cairo; meets contributors to *Personal Landscape*
	17 Nov.	Embarks for England and training for a new campaign
	mid-Dec.	Begins three weeks leave in England. Preparing selection and by January 1944 has 73 poems to give publisher

1944	Jan.–April	Training at Chippenham, Cambs., for European campaign
	February	Receives contract for poems; prepares illustrations for war narrative and for poems. Eleven days leave
	March	Chooses title *Bête Noire* for the selection; receives contract for war narrative
	4 April	Sends last poems to publisher
	6 April	Moves to top-security camp at Sway for final training in sea-borne invasion
	6 June	Commands a tank troop in main assault on Normandy beaches
	9 June	Killed near St Pierre

SCHOOL

MUMMERS

Put by your stitching. Spread the table
With winking cups and wines. That sable
Doff for your brighter silks: are all
Your glints of pearly laughter shuttered?
See where the outdoor snows, wind-fluttered,
Through the arched window fall.

See where the deep night's blast has straddled
The ancient gargoyle, weather-addled
And striped with melted tapestry
Of snow; his evil face well-carven
By Brother Ambrose, lean and starven,
Cell-fasting, rich in artistry.

Soon come the masked mummers, knocking
With hands snow-red. The door's unlocking
Answers the stars with indoor light.
Now to the drum tap, with snow-crusted
Cardboard steed, and ancient rusted
Blade, the Saint and Turk will fight.

1934

YOUTH

Your sword is brilliant: through the auburn leaves
The sun patches your tunic of smooth-woven green,
Each fold a thousand aery shimmers leaves,
Dazzling as leaping fish a moment seen.

The road curls down below you. In its spell
Pass glebe and woodland, where a hundred ways
Twist, some to fairyland, and some to Hell;
But there are better things beyond the maze.

When you have heard the whirl and song of strife,
When use scratches and rusts your weapons' gleam
And age has marred the youngness of your life
With dreams, you will come back again and dream.

[? 1935]

STRANGE GARDENER

Over the meadows
framed in the quiet osiers, dreams the pond;
region of summer gnat-busyness
and, in the afternoon's blue drowsiness,
plops among the water shadows:
and the cool trees wait beyond.

A young man lived there
with a swift, sad face, and full of phantasy,
repeating, as he heard it,
the alliterative speech of the water spirit;
smoothing his pale hair
with automatic ecstasy.

This was his garden
uncultivated (order hated him);
whence, in a winter madness
(whose scourge drove him to recklessness
seeing the frost harden),
the water spirit translated him.

[? 1935]

.303

I have looked through the pine-trees
Cooling their sun-warmed needles in the night,
I saw the moon's face, white,
    Beautiful as the breeze.

Yet you have seen the boughs sway with the night's breath,
Wave like dead arms, repudiating the stars
And the moon, circular and useless, pass
    Pock-marked with death.

Through a machine-gun's sights
I saw men curse, weep, cough, sprawl in their entrails;
You did not know The Gardener in the vales,
    Only efficiency delights you.

[? 1935]

BEXHILL

And, now in the South, the swallows
Are not known, not at this season, among these
Small streets and posters which the lamplight shews:
But are among the white-dusted avenues,
And where the ruined palace faces the green
Isonzo, the barbers chatter, the sky is clean.

[? 1935]

CARAVAN

Going beyond the gate they found these men
Sitting in the last light and regarding the great sun
With understanding. And one spoke to them presently,
Saying he had discovered the soul of music
At one time. And another said, that when
The birds flow southwards, heading across the continent,

Then the wild sea, under the always rhythmic
Shutter of wingtips, only suggests to spent
Eyes slanting, the slope of green and mountainous moving
Country; familiar, only no priests in the cities
Handling the cold bronze, counting. The stones in panic
Chilled, the bright dust reflecting the heavens' faces.

Thus he revealed the perfect sources, the lost
Wisdom, seeing only the loved existent;
The clouds flying, Earth stretching in silence
Chameleon, the colours limited, dyes all lost.
All this he told them, speaking the tongue of the swallows.

But they not knowing the words, nor in his hands
Seeing the meaning, went thence over the sands.

1935

IMAGES

The small men walk about antlike,
And the bell tolls. God created these
Beautiful or angular, not different.

The straight men are not there now
And their dark spears do not lean against the sun.
Not any more, since the bell has begun tolling.

The priests were acquainted with them,
Making chips in the pyramids,
At intervals in the warm stone.

The bell will go on tolling
To kings on their marble bases.
But these are the unacknowledged rulers.

And understanding the bell they do not hear it,
But walk over the hilltop
Into their rarer climate.

1935

FAMOUS MEN

And now no longer sung,
not mourning, not remembered
more under the sun,

not enough their deserved
praise. The quick movement of dactyls
does not compensate them.

The air is advertised of seas
they smote, from green to copper.
These were merciful men.

And think, like plates lie deep
licked clean their skulls,
rest beautifully, staring.

1935

DISTRACTION

Now my mind's off again. No tears
Of Catullus move me. Though I know in turn
We too will praise these years
Of watching clouds through windows, fluttering pages;
Usefully sometimes, though the beckoning scents
Rise always, wafted from summer grasses:
Hearing the loud bees mumble at the glass,
And sound of sunlight behind the scratching pens.

[? 1936]

ENCOUNTER WITH A GOD

Ono-no-komache the poetess
sat on the ground among her flowers,
sat in her delicate-patterned dress
thinking of the rowers,
thinking of the god Daikoku.

Thinking of the rock pool
and carp in the waterfall at night.
Daikoku in accordance with the rule
is beautiful, she said, with a slight
tendency to angles.

But Daikoku came
who had been drinking all night
with the greenish gods of chance and fame.
He was rotund standing in the moonlight,
with a round, white paunch.

Who said
I am not beautiful,
I do not wish to be wonderfully made,
I am intoxicated dutiful daughter,
and I will not be in a poem.

But the poetess sat still
holding her head and making verses:
'How intricate and peculiarly well-
arranged the symmetrical belly-purses
of lord Daikoku.'

1936

DEJECTION

Yesterday travellers in summer's country,
Tonight the sprinkled moon and ravenous sky
Say, we have reached the boundary. The autumn clothes
Are on. Death is the season and we the living
Are hailed by the solitary to join their regiment,
To leave the sea and the horses and march away
Endlessly. The spheres speak with persuasive voices.

Only tomorrow like a seagull hovers and cries:
The windows will be open and hearts behind them.

                                                    1936

A STORM

Curtaining this country the whispering rain
Stipples in cold monochrome the sun's
Alive and tinted picture, so warm once;
The wind's voice laden like reeds with random pain.

Impending with their frown the bowed trees,
Clouds make a ceiling by the rooks' village
At which how vainly they complain, silly
Voices fall down, lost in the day's disease.

Like all, this storm will blunder along the hills,
Retire muttering into a smutty corner
Of sky, and there dying, his rant stills.

Wait. See like a tired giant the sun return
To step into your valley and gladly fill
Evening with moist colour, made untarnished.

1936

VILLANELLE OF GORIZIA

Over and over the street is repeated with sunlight:
The oxen tire even of the leaves,
The flutes sound in the wineshop, out of sight.

The sky is apathetic like a kite
That cares not how the string below it weaves
Over and over; the street is repeated with sunlight

Till only doors are dark among the white
Walls that outstare the sun. And noon achieves
The flutes' sound in the wineshop, out of sight.

The town cannot remember when was night:
The trees droop for the subtle-coloured eves,
Over and over the street is repeated with sunlight.

The short shades of the avenues invite
The monk with his umbrella, who perceives
The flutes sound in the wineshop, out of sight.

O distant heat and music: if I might
Go back: after return my heart grieves.
Over and over the street is repeated with sunlight,
The flutes sound in the wineshop, out of sight.

1937

POINT OF VIEW

Old man or young man, if you are like me, like
to trace the turkish shadows on the down,
the busybody engine in the distance—
in your mind's ear the horses like a pistol
smack on the odd stone, rabble of winds at the hill's crown
egg them on. Or in the orchestra by the dyke

the chorus of reeds to talk when people have passed
saying they're gone they're gone, huddling like chums.
Yes if this is the sort of thing you want
or if you incline to sit indoors, and won't
step at the dusk's edge with seductive summer
but shut out the fields and read books too fast;

whichever it is, whichever ambition expands
across your horizon, or dream your soul enjoys;
if you are this, or if you wear that token,
who'll say, when Nurse has had her nap and woken,
who is to tell, when she takes away our toys
which of us will catch tears in his simple hand?

1937

KRISTIN

This season like a child on airy points
Has crept behind you in an evening time
To take you unawares and touch your hair
With a gift of gold. Or like a messenger
Arrives on the scene saying a god's wants,
To exile the dull colours and make us sublime.

Presently then our simple friend the sun
Will climb and watch out of his summer tower
To see us play this country interlude:
Love like the lovely plants he wants renewed—
Take it all back after the sun has gone
Perhaps—but humour him this candle hour.

Yes, futile to prolong this natural instant:
Black days lean over, hours curtailed with fear.
But look, while these flowers imbibe the rain
A little forlorn magic has homed again.
Take this, these limpid days will not be constant;
They will forsake you, will not reappear.

1937

ON LEAVING SCHOOL

Here where the years stand under us in the valley
We can look down upon their shops and vineyards
And honestly say we would rather be like leopards
Let out in one direction, who cannot be silly.

And at this evening moment, when the shallow
Echoes stagger against Big School, it is awkward
Realizing happiness seems just to have started
And now we must leave it, live like trees or charlock.

One of us will be the kettle past care of tinkers,
Rejected, one the tip-top apple, the winking
Sun's friend. It will be that way, and Time on our ground
Will sweep like a maid, and where we were be clean.
Shall we find room to laugh, if turning round
We see where we have walked, how wrong we have been?

1937

PLEASURES

Forgotten the red leaves painting the temple in summer,
Forgotten my squirrel in his dark chamber,
The great turtle and the catamaran;
Rivers, where the mosaic stones are found.

That church, amputated by high explosive,
Where priests no more lift up their murmurous Latin,
And only the sun, a solitary worshipper,
Tiptoes towards the altar and rests there.

These and the hazy tropic where I lived
In tall seas where the bright fish go like footmen
Down the blue corridors about their business—
The jewelled skulls are down there—I have forgotten,

Almost forgot. How slowly they return
Like princes into the rooms they once owned. How dimly
I see the imaginary moon, the magic painter
Of wide, deserted acres with splendour and silence.

Once on Monte Nero in the spring
Some peasant girl fashioned for love and work
Taught me a smile that I had forgotten.
It is so hard to speak that language now.

Almost forgot, how slowly they return
Like princes into the halls they once owned.

                                        1938

OXFORD

SPRING SAILOR

That high-decked cloud adventuring along
This day to anchor in the visionary
Night's land, has moved the birds with melody
Like kindly sirens to accompany
His silent voyage. Behold him now lie
Moored up beside the six trees, among

The islands of the sun, the distant isles.
And now the birds, the thriftless balladmongers,
Break off his tale, and begin to tell
The marvellous story without words, and still
Beyond your speech. These many skilful singers
Easily start your silly tears and smiles.

I will contrive to escape the dainty touch
Of a day so heavy with the imagery
Of longing. And the various eyes of Earth
Opening, the dreams ready for their rebirth,
Even the gentle hands of Earth for me
Shall move without disquieting me much.

1939

POOR MARY

Death has made up your face. His quiet hand
perfects your costume to impersonate
the one who cannot enter this living land.

And it is death who makes sure, and chances
no tenderness in the recesses of your eyes.
In the halls of your heart no spirit dances,

but you are the house of sorrow. In you all
colour is closed and casemented for ever;
no answering song inside the cold wall.

For to the travellers who cry, Death
come out and say why you are living here,
he will not answer. They have lost their breath.

Only an effigy bobbing at the pane
calls out with starling speech and falls down,
and there is silence in the house again.

1939

STRANGER

(For Y.C.S.)

What in the pattern of your face
Was writing to my eye, that journeyed once
Like an explorer in your beauty's land,
To find that venerable secret stand
Somehow carved there; and ever since
Has rested still, enchanted by the place?

Cast up along your eyes' dark shore
There, or within the cool red cave of lips,
My heart would spend a solitary spell,
Delighted hermit in his royal cell.
For your eyes and your precious mouth perhaps
Are blessed isles once found and found no more.

You are the whole continent of love
For me, the windy sailor on this ocean,
Who'd lose his ragged vessel to the waves
And call on you, the strange land, to save.
Here I set up my altar and devotion,
And let no storm blot out the place I have.

1939

INVADERS

Intelligences like black birds
come on their dire wings from Europe. Sorrows
fall like the rooks' clatter on house and garden.
And who will drive them back before we harden?
You will find, after a few tomorrows
like this, nothing will matter but the black birds.

You will not paint lips on your lips
or beautify yourself in anyone's eyes:
I shall never write a word to escape,
our life will take on a hard shape;
and then if we are spared we shall not arise
to hold the world up when it finally slips.

So keep a highlight in your handsome eye;
still be fastidious, and I will write
some well-intentioned words. To keep the heart
still sensitive as air will be our part,
always to think, and always to indite
of a good matter, while the black birds cry.

1939

PAS DE TROIS

Three dancers under music's orders stand
held by the touch of silence for a moment
posing. Now somewhere the flutes' sound
lifts the enchantment. Easily unbound,
they begin to move like plants and nod slowly
their three heads like blooms: their tendril hands

describe the shapes of air. The slender feet
on points of strength such as grass has,
gently to divide the strength of stone,
make them like gods miraculously borne:
Sonia, Tania, Katia, svelte deities
who sign to us and whom we may not greet.

Theirs is a craft of quiet,
they are shades of an old time
when you could hear, no riot
intervening, intricate and frail rhyme
and music; men had leisure
to ornament, only for pure pleasure,
their utensils and their life;
to live an hour or make a knife
intent on every jewelled space.

This is why they interlace
their fragile hands and dance their pace
of three before your ordinary face.

1939

DO NOT LOOK UP

Do not look up against this fluid sky;
though flames and Lucifer fall down again
you must persist in what we always said
while the strong march towards their usual bed.
Truth is your tongue and naturally remains
your study till the world's time to die.

If you default there may be none alert
to stop the heavy mould clamping on
lovers and children and the nascent hills;
none to awake the mazy people's wills
who are obedient to chaos, none
without you being skilful to avert

Death's logic. Closed in this imperilled earth
reflect, the dust and souls of merciful men
lie still. And not six feet above their rest
their poor successors go about to waste
the store of their amassing. Busy then
and harvest yet among a general dearth.

[?1939]

STARS

(For Antoinette)

The stars still marching in extended order
move out of nowhere into nowhere. Look, they are halted
on a vast field tonight, true no man's land.
Far down the sky with sword and belt must stand
Orion. For commissariat of this exalted
war-company, the Wain. No fabulous border

could swallow all this bravery, no band
will ever face them: nothing but discipline
has mobilized and still maintains them. So
Time and his ancestors have seen them. So
always to fight disorder is their business,
and victory continues in their hand.

From under the old hills to overhead,
and down there marching on the hills again
their camp extends. There go the messengers,
Comets, with greetings of ethereal officers
from tent to tent. Yes, we look up with pain
at distant comrades and plains we cannot tread.

[1939]

HAYDN—MILITARY SYMPHONY

Music creates two grenadiers, scarlet and tall
Leisurely fellows: in the long afternoon
They stroll with royal slow motion. How they twirl
Their regular canes. Each silly servant girl
Regards wide-eyed, or diffidently, soon
Is captured quite. The idle lords of all

The park, the dogs, the children, both wheel
Down the long walk between the lazy trees.
Yet scrutinize the regimental pair
And you will find, they are but men of air:
Their summer is a fantasy, and these
Like all authentic heroes are unreal.

Follow them none the less at the same pace:
For you perhaps to step behind these two
May shew such dead romances can revive,
The painted backcloth quicken and be alive.
You will look out upon this painted view
Of madmen in a non-existent place.

1939

HAYDN—CLOCK SYMPHONY

The timepiece standing butler in the hall
Beneath the remote ceiling, with the same
Grave air as Time himself, will let you pass
To quiz your elegant figure in a glass
And enter the long room. The brilliant game
Of dancing's at its height, the panic fall

And rise of music across the amazing floor
Where dresses, white dresses, sweep and dip
To the high notes as distant as the moon.
By a polite enchantment of the tune
Detained, step opposite some cherry lip,
Dark eye and oval countenance demure.

Consider, Sir, you move in eternity here:
No wonder you have the carriage of a god,
For here you are the one who in your sleep
Walks in the corridors and in the deep
Recesses of your mind: where you have trod
The polished ground of dreaming every year.

[1939]

TO A LADY ON THE DEATH
OF HER FIRST LOVE

So death, the adept subtle amorist,
Has taken from you what I might have kept
Fast in the queer casket of my heart.
You were beguiled to grant him that part
That was the whole of you. Then death crept
Like a secret jeweller, and the amethyst

That I diligently sought, he took and stored.
O rich man death, you sent your creature
From your demesne disguised with life, to steal
A gem you never wanted. You cannot feel
Its worth. And she, making the first gesture
Of waking, gave it you, the wicked lord.

It was death's emissary who took your love
To hoard it in the quiet land, nowhere.
He followed death's instructions from the start,
And when he had it of you, went apart
And tendered to his master death the fair
And gentle plunder. Death will keep it close enough.

Still I, the loving fool and last courtier
Attend you, and my service is still yours
For all the profit you enjoy of it.
Use my emotion and occasional wit
To colour each opaque hour, the course,
Despoiled princess, you must complete here.

[? 1939]

32

SANCTUARY

Once my mother was a wall;
behind my rampart and my keep
in a safe and hungry house
I lay as snug as winter mouse:
till the wall breaks and I weep
for simple reasons first of all.

All the barriers give in,
the world will lance at every point
my unsteady heart, still and still
to subjugate my tired will.
When it's done they will anoint me,
being kinder if they win.

So beyond a desperate fence
I'll cross where I shall not return,
the line between indifference
and my vulnerable mind:
no more then kind or unkind
touch me, no love nor hate burn.

1940

33

THE CREATOR

The unwearied sun from day to day
along his mathematic way
looks with an infant's eyes upon
what little in the world's not wrong;
and with no understanding tear
at the death of a sad year.

So he forgets and turns away west,
while with fine uninterest
and in bone-idle groups the stars
stupidly linger and watch pass
erupting woe and queasy mirth
across the sallow face of Earth.

So the Creator, with never less
ignorance of pity or remorse,
must gape at the eternal course
of sorrow, all His planning. Yes,
He's petrified, and cannot see
His marvellous inefficiency.

1940

VILLANELLE OF SUNLIGHT

The sunlight settled on a wall,
Magical traveller through the air,
Fills my heart with funerall

For all the dead who were the tall
Lovers and beauties, who found here
The sunlight settled on a wall.

They who were richest, they recall
None of their treasure. So despair
Fills my heart. With funerall

And with no usual mirth let fall
A sign of sorrow. Even fear
The sunlight settled on a wall.

For fear, that some which heard his call
Now are cold and do not care,
Fills my heart with funerall.

This sunlight, sojourner for all
These centuries, maintains his stare.
O, sunlight settled on a wall
Fills my heart with funerall.

[pub. March 1940]

GENDER RHYME

A man, a name of People, and a wind;
River and mountain feel them complete
The short journey to cavernous oblivion.

Man the little giant and the sweet
Bully hero has burst his entrails to defend
A People that's dead now. So the trivial

Wind blows over the hero and his kind
Over river and mountain to limbo in the end.

1940

RUSSIANS

How silly that soldier is pointing his gun at the wood:
he doesn't know it isn't any good.
You see, the cold and cruel northern wind
has frozen the whole battalion where they stand.

That's never a corporal: even now he's frozen
you can see he's only a commercial artist
whom they took and put those clothes on,
and told him he was one of the smartest.

Even now they're in ice it's easy to know
what a shock it's been, a long shock,
coming home to them wherever they go
with their mazed minds taking stock.

Walk among the innocuous parade
and touch them if you like, they're properly stayed:
keep out of their line of sight and they won't look.
Think of them as waxworks, or think they're struck

with a dumb immobile spell
to wake in a hundred years with the merry force
of spring upon them in the harmless world. Well,
at least don't think what happens when it thaws.

1940

FAREWELL POEM

Please, on a day falling in summer,
recall how being tired, you and I
among the idle branches by the river
and blind to propriety and passers-by,
where leaves like eyes turn sidelong to the river,
fell asleep embraced and let the shades run
half crossing us, and half the vigorous sun,
till he had almost climbed enough.

Because tired, what innocents we were,
protected by sleep you see we had not thought,
like a footprint before we were aware,
that day was complete behind us and wiped out:
so now we are broken apart unaware,
and keep pain prisoner cleverly enough.

Who is it that is pleased now we are sad,
who is satisfied and thanks his stars,
has got and has the happiness we had?
Will he enjoy long, or will the sudden alas,
and light-fingered sorrow pick his heart?
Of course: soon his misery will start,
for all delight is God's impermanent bluff.

In a minute he will come from the gold cloud,
the great black figure with a hideous laugh,
and hear the comfortable cry aloud;
the ethereal veil is cracked painted stuff,
and he will be backed with fires and the red cloud.
We must never start our story again;
for God is waiting with unexpended pain
and will not bless you my dark afflicted love.

1940

38

VILLANELLE OF SPRING BELLS

Bells in the town alight with spring
converse, with a concordance of new airs
make clear the fresh and ancient sound they sing.

People emerge from winter to hear them ring,
children glitter with mischief and the blind man hears
bells in the town alight with spring.

Even he on his eyes feels the caressing
finger of Persephone, and her voice escaped from tears
make clear the fresh and ancient sound they sing.

Bird feels the enchantment of his wing
and in ten fine notes dispels twenty cares.
Bells in the town alight with spring

warble the praise of Time, for he can bring
this season: chimes the merry heaven bears
make clear the fresh and ancient sound they sing.

All evil men intent on evil thing
falter, for in their cold unready ears
bells in the town alight with spring
make clear the fresh and ancient sound they sing.

1940

CANOE

Well, I am thinking this may be my last
summer, but cannot lose even a part of
pleasure in the old-fashioned art of
idleness. I cannot stand aghast

at whatever doom hovers in the background;
while grass and buildings and the somnolent river,
who know they are allowed to last for ever,
exchange between them the whole subdued sound

of this hot time. What sudden fearful fate
can deter my shade wandering next year
from a return? Whistle and I will hear
and come another evening, when this boat

travels with you alone towards Iffley:
as you lie looking up for thunder again,
this cool touch does not betoken rain;
it is my spirit that kisses your mouth lightly.

[pub. May 1940]

40

A ROUND NUMBER

The monotonous evil clock
is creeper climbing on my heart
and with rank ivy will pull down
my hope of happiness and renown.

My sacred lady without art
gives an idiot place to mock.

I know the fragrant girl is dead
and perished with my innocence
and died two hundred years ago
or twice that time if Time is slow,

and I think for recompense
she only lived inside my head.

Well she is gone: but I remember
my early promise, looking for
comfortable fame to make amends.
And here my last existence ends.

For I can't feed hope any more
and Time has reached a round number.

1940

A GOD IS BURIED

I

Turn your back on Monte Nero, that mountain
to the west. Turn your back on the white town
of Gorizia, plastered with notices and swarming
with soldiers. Cross the green Isonzo. Go down

by the ruined palace of the archbishop, the machine-gun schools,
and a company of the Alpini with their mules:
then uphill to where hundreds of saplings hide
where a generation of men and trees died:

and where the bright blood and shrapnel are sunk in grass
the golden oriole fluting in a cool hollow
colours the silence. These musical spirits pass
ahead and to the left. Now if you follow

you will come where high explosive could not move
the god who's buried in this flowering grove
but he has slept two hundred decades here.

No music will wake his marble. Not yet;
still he must rest in soil and forget
another madness begun this year.

II

Well, today there is a child outside who bows
and struts; some ritual of his invention.
And three hundred yards away the river moves
under the slowly moving sun: whoever loves
to know of this (and I am one), would hasten
to uncover the god from his dark house.
But listen to men talking and I would more
keep him with mountains where he was before.

III

White-limbed deity
in a cavity
of the safe earth, cased in,
lulled by a sound of the fertile
seed and sap working within
layers of ground close above you, while
that murderous plot gradually
heals and prepares for you to evacuate
your green shell, when you will youthfully
stamp the new earth with divine foot.
When you arise if I live I will hear the sound:
across Switzerland or Austria I will tread
whatever road; or dead, travel below ground
with the traditional despatch of the dead.

IV   The God answers:

Your words are not the first I have heard
trembling in the earth at long intervals
other voices have reached my dark bed
many have been here and departed,
scarcely have I passed the extremes of winter in
silence not broken by some mortal word.

At first I was tempted to indulge the hope
that of those reverent hands laid me here
where my divinity should outlive their doom
someone would escape and after years come
a happy messenger. Each year, each year
for generations I tried to hear his step.

But as the years like leaves perpetually
fell down to cover me and rot away
I turned to sleep, and you will come to agree
better a fathom sunk in darkness with me
whence with a profitable change you may
become a civilized and gentle tree.

1940

SHADOWS

Shadows are waters: in these forgetful caves
they stand or flow, purple and rich
on the rich earth. A dim tunnel of trees
wards off the whirling men and deities
from these involved corridors; that stretch
where memory easily makes graves

for dead sorrows, and has herself not long
to exist. Only thought swims about.
The sunlight filtering through leaves like glass
with flame purified will even pass
into the darkest channel of the moat.
But to the somnolent earth falls no song

or sound. It is sacrilege of course to speak,
but I am here for silence: I had heard
the property of this place to heal,
and I have come here not to feel
a wound winter and summer have not deterred
from aching. And I find this charm as weak.

1940

A MIME

Time and Death villains in the wings
stretch out their fingers parallel
at me. Death says: 'If I don't get you,
then Time aha will presently upset you—
you'll find how soon his famous spell
will coil you in successive strings.'

'But Sir,' says he, old melodramatic Death,
'May I be first one after all,
and Time young man will spare you, for
the young fill my fastidious maw
so tastily. Revel and grow tall,
rest you merry near your last breath.'

In deference to his advice
I look in maidens' faces after
what men cannot but need the most.
But Time as limber as a ghost
dispelling kisses and sweet laughter
looks to catch me in a trice.

Only between these dangerous two
I will be nimble, jump, and dodge
the unnatural uncles on my track;
if I don't croak and falter back
despairing in the end to cadge
careless hearts from you and you.

1940

THE DECEASED

He was a reprobate I grant
and always liquored till his money went.
His hair depended in a noose from
his pale brow. His eyes were dumb;
like prisoners in their cavernous slots, were
settled in attitudes of despair.
You who God bless you never sunk so low
censure and pray for him that he was so;
and with his failings you regret the verses
the fellow made, probably between curses,
probably in the extremes of moral decay,
but he wrote them in a sincere way:
and seems to have felt a sort of pain
to which your imagination cannot attain.

1940

SOISSONS

M. l'Épicier in his white hat
in an outhouse by the cathedral, makes
devils from the selfsame stone
men used in the religious century.
The cathedral itself in new masonry
of white, stands openly in this sunlit town,
Soissons. Down the long hill snakes
the hard hot road into the town's heart.

In the evening when the late sunlight abandons
buildings still glimmering from shadow on shadow
someone leans from a window eavesdropping our
strange voices so late in the cathedral square.
From the barracks of the 19th Regiment you can hear
the equivalent of Lights Out. Now the sweet-sour
wine clambers in our heads. Go in. Tomorrow
tiptoes with us along the dark landing.

'A Laon, belle cathédrale', making
a wave of his white hat, explains
the maker of gargoyles. So we take
a route for Laon and Rheims leaving you
Soissons, a simplified medieval view
taken from a Book of Hours. How dark
seems the whole country we enter. Now it rains,
the trees like ominous old men are shaking.

1940

SOISSONS 1940

This town is no tower of the mind
and the cathedral, not an edifice of air, stands
dignified and sleepy with serenity—
so I would have said, and that this solid city
was built here close under the angels' hands,
something we had no longer reckoned to find.

Yet here something of the mind lived and died,
a mental tower restored only to fall
and we in England heard it come down
as though of all, this was the most ominous sound.
The devils pilloried in that holy wall
must smile to see our faith broke to the wide.

You who believe you have a kind creator
are with your sire crowding into twilight,
as using excellent smooth instruments
material man makes himself immense.
Oh you may try, but can't deny he's right
and what he does and destroys makes him greater.

1940

ABSENCE

The long curtained French-windows conceal
the company at dinner by candlelight.
I am the solitary person on the lawn,
dressed up silver by the moon.
The bush on my left sleeps, the tree on my right
is awake but stays motionless to feel,

as I and Cupid on his ornament stone,
how the whole evening here discourses
and the stars too lean nearer to the earth,
for their traditional splendour pours forth
much more in such unpopulous places,
almost litters the trees like rain.

So the minutes assemble at first in silence
till here or there the speech of ghosts or leaves
is audible. And it appears each grieves,
the garden with its composite voice sighing:
She is not here, and you who come instead
shew by your attitude, she's dead.

1940

THE POETS

Once merchants, when the impassive sands
stare us out, and the sun, we long for towns—
but as we enter, the dealers spread their hands

in a gesture which means I have not,
not for you; mock us with obscenities or frowns.
In these settlements nothing, nothing is got

by strangers; nothing is accepted.
When we speak, even our words are bad
currency, to which they take exception.

And here, in squalid content
an ancient people lives. Is it not sad,
in a decade or two they'll be extinct.

But we ourselves are already phantoms;
boneless, substanceless, wanderers; they look at us
with primitive mistrust. The beggars and wantons

will not look, turn away. For we are hated,
known to be cursed, guessed to be venomous,
we must advance for ever, always belated.

[? 1940]

TO CURSE HER

You're handsome and false, and I could cover
that face with praise till I've stretched over
a figurative mask of words
for beauty; or my pen unloads
all that's packed up in the mind.
Then call a truce, and never find
enough, you are so fair, to do you honour.

The only voice to put with yours
Ulysses heard and strained the hawse
till it scarce held him to the sane mast—
I think your hair so glistened last
when Troilus found you in your uncle's hall,
jettisoned his arms with a humble gesture, fell
conquered, poor hero, in a deceitful house.

And if to portray you will exhaust
legends, illusion, eloquence, what most
will abash all my ingenuity
is doing justice to your perfidy.
Cressida could not match you, but I pray
you'll feel Cressida's ruin and decay
known for a strumpet, diseased and outcast.

1940

A BALLET

How cleverly the choreographer
and costumier combine—
the effects fine, and the young lady's line
impeccable. With what grace her arabesque
he caps with an entrechat, this stunningly dressed
young person, her partner.

All the colours of spring
they are dressed in,
they whirl about,
and the dance over, they gracefully leap out.

But here they come again, I'm certain, or
is this not the fair
young sylph? I declare
she has a dead face and a yellow eye
and he has no limbs—how dreadfully spry
he is on his stumps:
he bleeds, but he jumps
ten feet at a prance.
I don't like this dance.

1940

AN ORATION

In this city lovers, beneath this moon,
greater here than elsewhere, and more beautiful
who loves conspiracies and lovers, here you walked.
It was you who spoke in the dark streets, stood in the shadows
or where the lamps lit your white faces and red lips.
Yours were the figures which moved and disappeared
by the great dark church and the taciturn river:
many spirits stood there with you,
stood beside you and embraced, shadow with shadow,
when you kissed. Even the poor dead
who in despair entered the water at night
were there. They also acquiesced when you said:
this is our town because of what we experienced here.

Here the hucksters cried their swindles and bargains,
clothes, scent, and finery of all kinds
and here the balladmongers made their songs
many songs were composed, truth was recited,
the perfect utterance of several ages.

But it is no longer the jewel and setting for jewels
the ancient town in whose streets walked
centuries ago the saints and national heroes
where the divines taught, and the populace
dragged up great stones to build the white churches.
Then it was a golden age. With what sincerity
even those who were wrong lived. The beggars were proud
to be the beggars of this noble town.
Even then the foreigners came to learn, to admire
and in a time which some still remember
this was the city of amorists, collectors, and wits,
those among men to whom good things are given.
Consider then what sweet words and inventions
they spoke and thought, and yet though some still live
who knew these, the people themselves are dead,
wakeful and miserable in their dark graves.

Yes the dead are wakeful and swift, at once to know
when disgrace comes, strangers on their graves.
Meanwhile the living sleep like hogs
and in their sleep many strangers arrive
and they pathetically oblivious stand
imagining they are dreams; I cannot say
what they imagine, vain, impotent men.

But it is not irreparable. The city
may still stir, the city's soul become
alive, alive, and all her beauty alive;
the fountains playing in the squares, the white buildings
standing erect, smiling on the day,
and all the pleasant traffic moving again.
Songs will appear like flowers, they'll sing and sing
and everywhere as it used to be, permanent spring
for which this town was known, will fly and dance
on the soft air, the food and the wine flow
from all the fertile outskirts, plenty
for the poor and the rich, plenty for the admirers,
the visitors and those travelling through.
Such will the city be when she awakes.

This is not fine language or impossibility
but the happy people I paint for you today
who are yourselves unhappy, are yourselves.
You are the happy people, when you unswoon,
poor marionettes, when you become real.

1940

54

LEUKOTHEA

When you were alive, my Leukothea
your loveliness was not understood
and only I knew the processes
by which my ornament lived and breathed.
And when you died
I was persuaded to store you in the earth
and I remember when they put you there,
your too-expressive living eye
being covered by the dark eyelash,
and by its lid for a cerement.
At that moment those who looked at you
wondered I know how you could be made
in such exquisite material
and I would not explain for the world.
Even when they put the soil above you
they saw its unusual texture. The very grass
was a strange plant, precious as emeralds.

So all these years I have lived securely. I knew
I had only to uncover you
to see how the careful soil would have kept
all, as it was, untouched. I trusted the ground.
I knew the worm and the beetle would go by
and never dare batten on your beauty.

Last night I dreamed and found my trust betrayed
only the little bones and the great bones disarrayed.

1940

JOHN ANDERSON

John Anderson, a scholarly gentleman
advancing with his company in the attack
received some bullets through him as he ran.

So his creative brain whirled, and he fell back
in the bloody dust, (it was a fine day there
and warm). Blood turned his tunic black

while past his desperate final stare
the other simple soldiers run
and leave the hero unaware.

Apt epitaph or pun
he could not hit upon, to grace
a scholar's death; he only eyed the sun.

But I think, the last moment of his gaze
beheld the father of gods and men,
Zeus, leaning from heaven as he dies,

whom in his swoon he hears again
summon Apollo in the Homeric tongue:
Descend Phoebus and cleanse the stain

of dark blood from the body of John Anderson.
Give him to Death and Sleep,
who'll bear him as they can

out of the range of darts, to the broad vale
of Lycia; there lay him in a deep
solemn content on some bright dale.

And the brothers, Sleep and Death
lift up John Anderson at his last breath.

1940

Four Translations

HORACE: ODES I:V

What lissom boy among the roses,
Sprinkled with liquid scents, proposes
To court you in your grotto, fair
Pyrrha? For whom is your blond hair

Bound, with plain art? Alas, how often
Will he bid changed gods to soften,
Till, poor landlubber, he finds
The sea so rough with inky winds:

Who now, poor gull, enjoys you gold
And always careless, always bold
To love, hopes on and never knows
The gold is tinsel. Sad are those

For whom you shine, untried. For me,
Beholden to the great god of the sea
A votive tablet will recall
Drenched garments on his temple wall.

1940

LE DORMEUR DU VAL

(From the French of Arthur Rimbaud. 1870)

It is a hollow of verdure with a brook singing
which distractedly with rags of silver arrays
the grass; where the sun in pride across the mountain
sparkles. It is a vale effervescent with rays.

A young soldier with bare head and mouth open
and his neck immersed in the fresh blue flowers
is sleeping stretched out in grass under heaven
pale in his green bed where the light showers.

His feet in swordgrass, he sleeps smiling. So
smiles a sick child. He is fallen in a doze.
Nature, attend and warm him, he is cold.

These scents will not succeed to charm
his nostrils. Asleep in sunlight with his arm
across him. On the right side are two red holes.

[pub. April 1940]

AU CABARET-VERT

(From the French of Arthur Rimbaud)

For eight days I had worn my boots out
on the cobbles of streets. I entered Charleroi
and at the Cabaret-Vert bespoke a cut
of bread and butter, some warm ham, no more.

Content, I stretched my legs under the green table
and contemplated the ingenuous designs
of the carpet. Also it was delectable
when the girl with the enormous breasts and sparkling eyes—

she wouldn't be frightened of a kiss, that girl—
brought me my bread and butter all with a smile,
some warm ham in a decorated plate,

some pink and white ham, touched with a perfume
of garlic: and filled me a great glass, its foam
gilt with a glimmer of belated sunlight.

[pub. May 1940]

HEAD OF A FAUN

(From the French of Arthur Rimbaud)

In the foliage, a green casket spotty with gold,
In the green foliage indefinite and flowery
With splendid flowers where a kiss is curled
Alive, and bursts their exquisite embroidery,

A wild faun shews his two eyes
And bites, in his white teeth, the red flowers:
Tanned and full-blooded as an ancient wine,
Under the branches his lip curls in laughters.

And when like a squirrel he has run away free,
His laughter yet trembles on every leaf.
Made finer by the bullfinch you may see
The bosky golden kiss in new relief.

1940

ARMY: ENGLAND

AN EXERCISE AGAINST IMPATIENCE

This city experiences a difficult time. The old bells
fall silent, or are bidden to silence. The buildings lean
inwards, watching the questionable sky,
and across the meadows, where youth and age inhabit
exchange an austere opinion of foreboding.

This tremor must be sensible even to ghosts
of whom there are many here and there, travelling
carefully to and fro. They also question
perhaps, gesturing with their paper hands.

But all these whom wisdom and no curse keeps
in a kind of existence beyond their ordinary time here;
they must know how thought still works,
a hidden creator like the silkworm. It is this
to which I cling, and think will save us all.

For does not the tree stand, the broad hill
scarred by no worse wounds than before
he could sustain
and can easily resist again?
The colossal ocean on his crusty floor
is ordered by his influences still
and all the lights with mild simplicity shine
and clouds and atmosphere are the same
as they have been;
the seven winds, serene
or blusterous, as their nature is wild or tame
move from their quarters and return again.
And in this circle caught
spirits of every gentle sort
are in the heart
of every element, its richest part,
imprisoned: for at present taught
to abide motionless, they await their round.

Meanwhile these signs are not of the world's end,
it is another famous age they portend.

The work will be
for us now, only to wait:
then in the chaotic state
tomorrow, we can set these spirits free.

Even, we will command and wield
good forces. And if we die? And if we die
those we have met or heard of will not be cold
they are as suitable as you and I.

Army Equitation School, Weedon, 1940

THE NEWS FROM EARTH

The limber monsters of the deep
quickening from an age of sleep
move in their dim viridian country
and soon, soon many a masthead sentry
will view Leviathan, like a continent, keep

the horizon to the North:
South all the humane porpoises dance forth,
sea nymphs and mermaidens with every scale
jewelled from the depth, lead on the ponderous whale
with musical and watery mirth.

And every luxurious beast with purple eye
in the hot East you shall espy
his second ornamental age begin.
See with alchemic horn and golden skin
the heraldic Unicorn at leisure lie.

Sweet Zephyr also swims
down the soft air to meet his comrades. Pan begins
to address his pipe, unused to sing for years
and every hydrant deity uprears
with merry sound of splash his weedy limbs.

Out of the constellations all the Gods
leap down upon the mountains' cloudy heads
and all the unbending hills smile when
Bacchus at last conveys the news to men
and Cupid again leads lusty youth to bed.

Army Equitation School, Weedon, 1940

EXTENSION TO
FRANCIS THOMPSON

Look in earth and air to catch
his mineral or electric eye.
And in the universe his voice
assumes perfect diversity.

The natural laws his angels are
and circumspectly go about
leaving marks the learned know
one for man to follow out.

Leo in drawing Deirdre's lips
drew as hand and pen were sent
by heaven. This perfection slips
through the hands to the instrument.

Expert diplomats' good taste
the curious statement of a child
or in his enamelled case
the doughty beetle hard and wild.

All in different degrees
embody the celestial thing
and the wise man will learn of these
analysis in worshipping.

[pub. January 1941]

THE PRISONER

Today, Cheng, I touched your face
with two fingers, as a gesture of love,
for I can never prove enough
by sight or sense your strange grace;

but like moths my hands return
to your skin, that's luminous
like a lamp in a paper house,
and touch, to teach love and learn.

I think a thousand hours are gone
that so, like gods, we'd occupy:
but alas, Cheng, I cannot tell why,
today I touched a mask stretched on the stone-

hard face of death. There was the urge
to escape the bright flesh and emerge
of the ambitious cruel bone.

Royal Military College, Sandhurst, 1940

OXFORD

At home, as in no other city, here
summer holds her breath in a dark street
the trees nocturnally scented, lovers like moths
go by silently on the footpaths
and spirits of the young wait
cannot be expelled, multiply each year.

In the meadows, walks, over the walls
the sunlight, far-travelled, tired and content,
warms the recollections of old men, touching
the hand of the scholar on his book, marching
through quadrangles and arches, at last spent
it leans through the stained windows and falls.

This then is the city of young men, of beginning,
ideas, trials, pardonable follies,
the lightness, seriousness and sorrow of youth.
And the city of the old, looking for truth,
browsing for years, the mind's seven bellies
filled, become legendary figures, seeming

stones of the city, her venerable towers;
dignified, clothed by erudition and time.
For them it is not a city but an existence;
outside which everything is a pretence:
within, the leisurely immortals dream,
venerated and spared by the ominous hours.

Army, Oxford, 1941

THE HOUSE

I am a pillar of this house
of which it seems the whole is glass
likewise transparent to the touch
for men like weightless shadows march
ignorantly in at the bright portico
or through a wall serenely go
unnoticing: myself am like a mouse
and carefully inspect all those that pass.

I am the pillar about which
like a conjured spectacle, such
amazing walls and floors appeared
as in the house that devils made.
Yet this queer magnificence
shows not to many, its defence
not being walls but in the property
that it is thin as air and hard to see.

I am the pillar and again the one
walking a perpetual up-and-down
scrutinizing all these
substances, shadows on their ways
crowding or evacuating the place.
At times a voice singing, or a face
may seem suspended in the cunning air;
a voice by itself, a face traversing the stair
alone, like a mask of narrow porcelain.
These I introduce but lose again
which are of the imagination, or of air,
being in relation to the house, actually there
yet unreal till I meet with one
who has that creative stone
to turn alive, to turn all alive:
prospecting this is all the care I have.

In order of appearance chosen by chance
whether to speak, to sing, to play, or dance
to my mute invisible audience
many have performed here and gone hence.
Some have resided in the house a time
the best rooms were theirs, also for them
scents and decorations were introduced
and other visitors were refused.
But when for weeks, months no one came near
an unpleasant prompting of suspicious fear
sent me climbing up to inspect the high
attic, where I made a curious discovery.
In this room which I had not entered for months
among the old pictures and bowls for hyacinths
and other refuse, I discovered the body
conventionally arranged, of a young lady
whom I admit I knew once, but had heard
declined in another country and there died.

Here's the strange fact, for here she lies.
If I but raise them my incredulous eyes
discern her, fairer now than when she lived
because on death her obscure beauty thrived;
the eyes turned to fine stones, the hair to flexible
gold, her flesh to the most natural marble,
until she's the most permanent thing
in this impermanent building
and to remove her I must use
some supernatural device
it seems: for I am forced to say
she arrived in a miraculous way.
I never studied such things; it will need a wiser
practitioner than me to exorcize her
but till the heart is dust and the gold head
disintegrates, I shall never hear the tread
of the visitors at whom I cannot guess,
the beautiful strangers, coming to my house.

Wickwar, Glos., 1941

TIME EATING

Ravenous Time has flowers for his food
at Autumn—yet can cleverly make good
each petal: devours animals and men,
but for ten dead he can create ten.

If you enquire how secretly you've come
to mansize from the bigness of a stone
it will appear it's his art made you rise
so gradually to your proper size.

But while he makes he eats: the very part
where he began, even the elusive heart
Time's ruminative tongue will wash
and slow juice masticate all flesh.

That volatile huge intestine holds
material and abstract in its folds:
thought and ambition melt, and even the world
will alter, in that catholic belly curled.

But Time, who ate my love, you cannot make
such another. You who can remake
the lizard's tail and the bright snakeskin
cannot, cannot. That you gobbled in
too quick: and though you brought me from a boy
you can make no more of me, only destroy.

Wickwar, Glos., 1941

SONG

Dotards do not think
but slowly slowly turn
eyes that have seen too much
expecting the soft touch
of Fate who cannot burn
but is a last drink,
a night drink, an opiate,
and almost comes too late.

I who could feel pain
a month, a month ago
and pleasure for my mind
and other pleasure find
like any dotard now
am wearily sat down,
a dull man, a prisoner
in a dull chamber.

You who richly live
look at me, look at me;
stirred to talk with you
I speak a word or two
like an effigy.
What answer will you give?
Can you wake the drugged man?
I wonder if you can.

Wickwar, Glos., 1941

THE MARVEL

A baron of the sea, the great tropic
swordfish, spreadeagled on the thirsty deck
where sailors killed him, in the bright Pacific

yielded to the sharp enquiring blade
the eye which guided him and found his prey
in the dim country where he was a lord;

which is an instrument forged in semi-darkness
yet taken from the corpse of this strong traveller
becomes a powerful enlarging glass

reflecting the unusual sun's heat.
With it a sailor writes on the hot wood
the name of a harlot in his last port.

For it is one most curious device
of many, kept by the interesting waves—
and I suppose the querulous soft voice

of mariners who rotted into ghosts
digested by the gluttonous tides
could recount many. Let them be your hosts

and take you where their forgotten ships lie
with fishes going over the tall masts—
all this emerges from the burning eye.

And to engrave that word the sun goes through
with the power of the sea,
writing her name and a marvel too.

Linney Head, Wales, [May] 1941

SIMPLIFY ME WHEN I'M DEAD

Remember me when I am dead
and simplify me when I'm dead.

As the processes of earth
strip off the colour and the skin
take the brown hair and blue eye

and leave me simpler than at birth
when hairless I came howling in
as the moon came in the cold sky.

Of my skeleton perhaps
so stripped, a learned man will say
'He was of such a type and intelligence,' no more.

Thus when in a year collapse
particular memories, you may
deduce, from the long pain I bore

the opinions I held, who was my foe
and what I left, even my appearance
but incidents will be no guide.

Time's wrong-way telescope will show
a minute man ten years hence
and by distance simplified.

Through that lens see if I seem
substance or nothing: of the world
deserving mention or charitable oblivion

74

not by momentary spleen
or love into decision hurled
leisurely arrive at an opinion.

Remember me when I am dead
and simplify me when I'm dead.

[? May 1941]

75

[Handwritten annotations, left:] repetition of final verse represents cicle of life — we come into this world the same way we leave it = helpless and afraid — repetition of his wishes = saying do not overcomplicate

[Handwritten annotations, right:] does not want love or shock to lead him people to praise him as people often exaggerate their feeling when someone passes, but then that death is forgotten He would rather be remembered ?? past his death by those who really care about him

ARMY: MIDDLE EAST

SONG

Do I venture away too far
from the hot coast of your love
whose southern virtues charmed me?
How long how long can I be safe,
for the poisonous sea and a cruel star
the one by day and one at night have charmed me.

And are you troubled with a fear
that I must be a seastruck lad
or that the devil armed me
with a compass in my head?
For the poisonous sea and a cruel star
the one by day and one at night have charmed me.

At night I see the hissing fire
when star and sea communicate
and they have alarmed me
by their interest and hate
for the poisonous sea and a cruel star
the one by day and one at night have charmed me.

O listen to the ship and hear
she sings all night a sailors' rune;
since the green water's claimed me
harm is coming to her soon
for the poisonous sea and a cruel star
the one by day and one at night have charmed me.

Yes, for I am doomed my dear
and I have jilted myself and you;
soon when the sea's embalmed me
I'll fade into the deceitful blue,
for the poisonous sea and a cruel star
the one by day and one at night have charmed me.

Cairo 12 September 1941

THE TWO VIRTUES

Love me, and though you next experiment
with Arabian books, or search the exact centre
and the limit of love's continent
with an orator, a dancer, or a sailor
there's none so fierce as I nor so inconstant.
I've the two virtues of a lover
hot as the Indies, mutable as weather.

Hot, since of his own heat must
the lover touch you to a flame
firing the heart and its imprisoning dust
like saints, to be in heaven when they burn
reciprocating heat; alight remain
until the flames die out above
the dying salamander, love.

Then being true to love, I'll be inconstant;
not to be so, would cheat you of the last
and most of love, sorrow's violent
and rich effect. In that lagoon the lost,
the drowned heart is wonderfully recast
and made into a marvel by the sea,
that stone, that jewel tranquillity.

Sarafand [September] 1941

NEGATIVE INFORMATION

As lines, the unrelated symbols of
nothing you know, discovered in the clouds
idly made on paper, or by the feet of crowds
on sand, keep whatever meaning they have

and you believe they write, for some
intelligence, messages of a sort;
these curious indentations on my thought
with every week, almost with each hour come.

Perhaps you remember the fantastic moon
in the Atlantic—we descried the prisoner laden
with the thornbush and lantern—
the phosphorescence, the ship singing a sea-tune.

How we lost our circumstances that night
and, like spirits attendant on the ship
now at the mast, now on the waves, might almost dip
and soar as lightly as our entranced sight.

Against that, the girls who met us at one place
were not whores, but women old and young at once
whom accidents turned to pretty stones,
to images alight with deceptive grace.

And in general, the account of many deaths—
whose portents, which should have undone the sky,
had never come—is now received casually.
You and I are careless of these millions of wraiths.

For as often as not we meet
in dreams our own dishevelled ghosts;
and opposite, the modest hosts
of our ambition stare them out.

To this, there's no sum I can find—
the hungry omens of calamity
mixed with good signs, and all received with levity,
or indifference, by the amazed mind.

Palestine, 16 October 1941

THE HAND

The hand is perfect in itself—the five
fingers though changing attitude depend
on a golden point, the imaginary true focal
to which infinities of motion and shape are yoked.
There is no beginning to the hand, no end,
and the bone retains its proportion in the grave.

I can transmute this hand, changing each
finger to a man or a woman, and the hills
behind, drawn in their relation:
and to more than men, women, hills, by alteration
of symbols standing for the fingers, for the whole hand,
this alchemy is not difficult to teach,

this making a set of pictures; this drawing
shapes within the shapes of the hand—
an ordinary translation of forms. But hence,
try to impose arguments
whose phrases, each upon a digit, tend
to the centre of reasoning, the mainspring.

To do this is drilling the mind, still a recruit,
for the active expeditions of his duty
when he must navigate alone the wild
cosmos, as the Jew wanders the world:
and we, watching the tracks of him at liberty
like the geometry of feet
upon a shore, constructed in the sand,
look for the proportions, the form of an immense hand.

Nathanya, Palestine, [October] 1941

ADAMS*

Walking alone beside the beach
where the Mediterranean turns in sleep
under the cliffs' demiarch,

walking thinking slowly I see
a dead bird and a live bird
the dead eyeless, but with bright eye

the live bird discovered me
stepping from a black rock into the air:
leave the dead bird to lie. Watch him fly

electric, brilliant blue
beneath he is orange, like flame—
colours I can't believe are so;

as legendary flowers bloom
incendiary in tint, a focal point
like Adams in a room.

Adams is like a bird
alert (high on his pinnacle of air
he does not hear you, someone said);

in appearance he is bird-eyed,
the bones of his face are
like the hollow bones of a bird.

And he stood by the elegant wall
between two pictures hanging there
certain of homage from us all

as through the mind this minute
he draws the universe
and, like our admiration, dresses in it

towering like the cliffs of this coast
with his stiletto wing
and orange on his breast:

he sucked up, utterly drained
the colour of my sea,
the yellow of this tidal ground,

swallowing my thought
swallows all those dark fish there
that a rock hides from sunlight.

Till Rest, cries my mind to Adams' ghost;
only go elsewhere, let me alone
creep into the dead bird, cease to exist.

Nathanya, [Palestine, October] 1941

---

* See related poem 'The Sea Bird', and note, p. 151.

THE SEA BIRD

Walking along beside the beach
where the Mediterranean turns in sleep
under the cliffs' demiarch

through a curtain of thought I see
a dead bird and a live bird
the dead eyeless, but with a bright eye

the live bird discovered me
and stepped from a black rock into the air—
I turn from the dead bird to watch him fly,

electric, brilliant blue,
beneath he is orange, like flame,
colours I can't believe are so,

as legendary flowers bloom
incendiary in tint, so swift he
searches about the sky for room,

towering like the cliffs of this coast
with his stiletto wing
and orange on his breast:

he has consumed and drained
the colours of the sea
and the yellow of this tidal ground

till he escapes the eye, or is a ghost
and in a moment has come down
crept into the dead bird, ceased to exist.

[pub. January 1943]

86

THESE GRASSES, ANCIENT ENEMIES*

These grasses, ancient enemies
waiting at the edge of towns,
conceal a movement of live stones,
the lizards with hooded eyes
of hostile miraculous age.

It is not snow on the green spurs
of hilltops, only towns of white
whose trees are populous with fruit;
with girls whose velvet beauty is
handed down to them, gentle ornaments.

Somewhere in the hard land
and vicious scrub, or fertile place
of women and productive trees
you think you see a devil stand
fronting a creature of good intention

or fair apples where the snake plays—
don't you? Sweet leaves but poisonous,
or a mantrap in a gay house
a murderer with a lover's face
seem to you the signs of this country?

But devil and angel do not fight,
they are the classic Gemini
for whom it's vital to agree
whose interdependent state
this two-faced country reflects. Curiously

though foreigners we surely shall
prove this background's complement
the kindly visitors who meant
so well all winter but at last fell
unaccountably to killing in the spring.

[Syria, November 1941]

* See related poem 'Syria', and note, p. 151.

SYRIA

These grasses, ancient enemies
waiting at the edge of towns
conceal a movement of live stones,
the lizards with hooded eyes
of hostile miraculous age.

It is not snow on the green space
of hilltops, only towns of white
whose trees are populous with fruit
and girls whose velvet beauty is
handed down to them, gentle ornaments.

Here I am a stranger clothed
in the separative glass cloak
of strangeness. The dark eyes, the bright-mouthed
smiles, glance on the glass and break
falling like fine strange insects.

But from the grass, the inexorable lizard,
the dart of hatred for all strangers finds
in this armour, proof only against friends,
breach after breach, and like the gnat is busy
wounding the skin, leaving poison there.

[? November 1941–June 1942]

EGYPTIAN SENTRY, CORNICHE, ALEXANDRIA

Sweat lines the statue of a face
he has; he looks at the sea
and does not smell its animal smell
does not suspect the heaven or hell
in the mind of a passer-by:
sees the moon shining on a place

in the sea, leans on the railing, rests
a hot hand on the eared rifle-muzzle,
nodding to the monotone of his song
his tarbush with its khaki cover on.
There is no pain, no pleasure, life's no puzzle
but a standing, a leaning, a sleep between the coasts

of birth and dying. From mother's shoulder
to crawling in the rich gutter, millionaire of smells,
standing, leaning at last with seizing limbs
into the gutter again, while the world swims
on stinks and noises past the filthy wall
and death lifts him to the bearer's shoulder.

The moon shines on the modern flats
where sentient lovers or rich couples
lie loving or sleeping after eating.
In the town the cafés and cabarets seating
gossipers, soldiers, drunkards, supple
women of the town, shut out the moon with slats.

Everywhere is a real or artificial race
of life, a struggle of everyone to be
master or mistress of some hour.
But of this no scent or sound reaches him there.
He leans and looks at the sea:
sweat lines the statue of a face.

[? Alexandria, July–August 1942]

L'AUTOBUS

The motorbus in the Rue Malika Nazli
motorbus of the School of the Incarnation
making bulldog grunts in its nose
turns out into the Saturday traffic whose
diverging streams embrace the white policeman.
The twenty-six young girls stare busily

conjecturing, twittering, out of eyes
black, grey, brown, violet, nocturnal blue
of a dozen countries. Their mothers' mothers were
perhaps Odysseus' bondwomen, the fair
women of the Troad, Tunisians, Syrians who
for centuries mingled with the swarthy coastwise

seamen, variegated women of the ports
and seabounded villages of many tongues
among the gulls' cries. Probably eyed ships
carried these children's ancestors on trade trips
among the wine-dark sea's white towns
famous for beauty and nefarious arts.

Now under the nun's eye they sit,
the neutralizing beam of holiness;
their touring eyes, ignorant of love or pain
to come, watch eagerly the intriguing game,
street counterplay of virtue and wickedness
in which their mothers were so versed, so adept.

[? *Alexandria, July–August 1942*]

DEVILS

My mind's silence is not that of a wood
warm and full of the sun's patience,
who peers through the leaves waiting
perhaps the arrival of a god,
silence I welcomed when I could:
but this deceptive quiet is
the fastening of a soundproof trap
whose idiot crew must not escape.
Only within they make their noise;
all night, against my sleep, their cries.
Outside the usual crowd of devils
are flying in the clouds, are running
on the earth, imperceptibly spinning
through the black air alive with evils
and turning, diving in the wind's channels.
Inside the unsubstantial wall
these idiots of the mind can't hear
the demons talking in the air
who think my mind void. That's all;
there'll be an alliance of devils if it fall.

[? Egypt, August 1942]

92

EGYPT

Aniseed has a sinful taste:
at your elbow a woman's voice
like I imagine the voice of ghosts,
demanding food. She has no grace

but, diseased and blind of an eye
and heavy with habitual dolour
listlessly finds you and I
and the table, are the same colour.

The music, the harsh talk, the fine
clash of the drinkseller's tray
are the same to her as her own whine,
she knows no variety.

And in fifteen years of living
found nothing different from death
but the difference of moving
and the nuisance of breath.

A disguise of ordure can't hide
her beauty, succumbing in a cloud
of disease, disease, apathy. My God,
the king of this country must be proud.

[Egypt, ? September 1942]

CHRISTODOULOS

Christodoulos moves, and shakes
his seven chins. He is that freak
a successful alchemist, and makes
God knows how much a week.

Out of Christodoulos' attic,
full of smoke and smells, emerge
soldiers like ants; with ants' erratic
gestures seek the pavement's verge;

weak as wounded, leaning in a knot
shout in the streets for an enemy—
the dross of Christodoulos' pot
or wastage from his alchemy.

They flow elsewhere; by swarthy portals
entering the crucibles of others
and the lesser sages' mortars:
but Christodoulos is the father

of all, he's the original wise one
from whose experiments they told
how War can be the famous stone
for turning rubbish into gold.

[Egypt, ? September 1942]

THE KNIFE

Can I explain this to you? Your eyes
are entrances the mouths of caves.
I issue from wonderful interiors
upon a blessed sea and a fine day,
from inside these caves I look and dream.

Your hair explicable as a waterfall
in some black liquid cooled by legend
fell across my thought in a moment
became a garment I am naked without
lines drawn across through morning and evening.

And in your body each minute I died
moving your thigh could disinter me
from a grave in a distant city:
your breasts deserted by cloth, clothed in twilight
filled me with tears, sweet cups of flesh.

Yes, to touch two fingers made us worlds
stars, waters, promontories, chaos
swooning in elements without form or time
come down through long seas among sea marvels
embracing like survivors on our islands.

This I think happened to us together
though now no shadow of it flickers in your hands
your eyes look down on ordinary streets
if I talk to you I might be a bird
with a message, a dead man, a photograph.

[Wadi Natrun, October 1942]

I LISTEN TO THE DESERT WIND

I listen to the desert wind
that will not blow her from my mind;
the stars will not put down a hand,
the moon's ignorant of my wound

moving negligently across
by clouds and cruel tracts of space
as in my brain by nights and days
moves the reflection of her face.

Like a bird my sleepless eye
skims the sands who now deny
the violent heat they have by day
as she denies her former way

all the elements agree
with her, to have no sympathy
for my impertinent misery
as wonderful and hard as she.

O turn in the dark bed again
and give to him what once was mine
and I'll turn as you turn
and kiss my swarthy mistress pain.

Wadi Natrun, [October] 1942

96

THE OFFENSIVE 1

Tonight's a moonlit cup
and holds the liquid time
that will run out in flame,
in poison we shall sup.

The moon's at home in a passion
of foreboding. Her lord
the martial sun, abroad
this month will see Time fashion

the design we begin:
and Time will cage again
the devils we let run
whether we lose or win.

Till in the month's dregs will
a month hence, some descry
the too late prophecy
of what the month lets fall.

This overture of quiet
is a minute to think on
the quiet like a curtain
when the piece is complete.

So in conjecture stands
my starlit body. The mind
mobile as a fox goes round
the sleepers waiting for their wounds.

This overture of quiet
is a minute to think on
the quiet like a curtain
when the piece is complete.
                    [Wadi Natrun, October 1942]

THE OFFENSIVE 2*

The stars are dead men in the sky
who will applaud the way you die:
the easy sun
won't criticize or carp because
after the death of many heroes
evils remain.

When you are dead and the harm done
the orators and clerks go on
the fishlike rulers of interims and wars
are as effete and useless as stars.

The stars are people in a house of glass
the heavenly representatives of a class
dead in their seats
the sun officially goes round
organizing life: and all he's planned
Time subtly eats.

The sun, the sun and the stars go round
the nature of eternity is circular
take as long as you like to find
all our successes and failures are similar.

We shall discover, if we should stand again
in Europe, Egypt, America, looking in vain
extending, expanding,
the orators dropping down a curtain of rhetoric,
behind which the actors retire, the heroic
action is ending.

[Wadi Natrun, October 1942–Tripolitania, January 1943]

* In some versions 'The Offensive 1' and 'The Offensive 2', are
presented as a single poem in two parts; see note, pp. 152–3.

MERSA

This blue halfcircle of sea
moving transparently
on sand as pale as salt
was Cleopatra's hotel:

here is a guesthouse built
and broken utterly, since.
An amorous modern prince
lived in this scoured shell.

Now from the skeletal town
the cherry skinned soldiers stroll down
to undress to idle on the white beach.
Up there, the immensely long road goes by

to Tripoli: the wind and dust reach
the secrets of the whole
poor town whose masks would still
deceive a passer-by;

faces with sightless doors
for eyes, with cracks like tears
oozing at corners. A dead tank alone
leans where the gossips stood.

I see my feet like stones
underwater. The logical little fish
converge and nip the flesh
imagining I am one of the dead.

[after October 1942]

Handwritten annotations:

history repeating itself → war imagery

images of peacefulness, calm

el-malnourished – starving – lacking vitality

shows vulnerability (to sun, nature)

don't peacefulness

poor, no personal contact, detached, ghost

own sun-burnt

poor town, exposed, malnourished

stripped down to its bare bones

being care-free, no worries

looks like a town, there's people in it

tears weeping

continuation of the idea of the mind, everything is decaying

juxtaposition between person the old and new reality

they're the wrong people — the original people have been displaced

time passing, time of the day onomatopoeia

foreshadowing his own death by repeating the word "I"

no emotion, practically, opposite

idea of poem is that we all die and death is inevitable, fatalism → acceptance of death

they know he will die or gonna die already is

99

DEAD MEN

Tonight the moon inveigles them
to love: they infer from her gaze
her tacit encouragement.
Tonight the white dresses and the jasmin scent
in the streets. I in another place
see the white dresses glimmer like moths. Come

to the west, out of that trance, my heart—
here the same hours have illumined
sleepers who are condemned or reprieved
and those whom their ambitions have deceived;
the dead men, whom the wind
powders till they are like dolls: they tonight

rest in the sanitary earth perhaps
or where they died, no one has found them
or in their shallow graves the wild dog
discovered and exhumed a face or a leg
for food: the human virtue round them
is a vapour tasteless to a dog's chops.

All that is good of them, the dog consumes.
You would not know, now the mind's flame is gone,
more than the dog knows: you would forget
but that you see your own mind burning yet
and till you stifle in the ground will go on
burning the economical coal of your dreams.

Then leave the dead in the earth, an organism
not capable of resurrection, like mines,
less durable than the metal of a gun,
a casual meal for a dog, nothing but the bone
so soon. But tonight no lovers see the lines
of the moon's face as the lines of cynicism.

And the wise man is the lover
who in his planetary love revolves
without the traction of reason or time's control
and the wild dog finding meat in a hole
is a philosopher. The prudent mind resolves
on the lover's or the dog's attitude for ever.

[pub. March 1943]

AE
BE
CE
CE
BE
AE

envelope
rhyme
scheme

image of fish

link to

"Mesa"

melancholic imagery

CAIRO JAG

Shall I get drunk or cut myself a piece of cake,
a pasty Syrian with a few words of English
or the Turk who says she is a princess—she dances
apparently by levitation? Or Marcelle, Parisienne
always preoccupied with her dull dead lover:
she has all the photographs and his letters
tied in a bundle and stamped *Décédé* in mauve ink.
All this takes place in a stink of jasmin.

But there are the streets dedicated to sleep
stenches and the sour smells, the sour cries
do not disturb their application to slumber
all day, scattered on the pavement like rags
afflicted with fatalism and hashish. The women
offering their children brown-paper breasts
dry and twisted, elongated like the skull,
Holbein's signature. But this stained white town
is something in accordance with mundane conventions—
Marcelle drops her Gallic airs and tragedy
suddenly shrieks in Arabic about the fare
with the cabman, links herself so
with the somnambulists and legless beggars:
it is all one, all as you have heard.

But by a day's travelling you reach a new world
the vegetation is of iron
dead tanks, gun barrels split like celery
the metal brambles have no flowers or berries
and there are all sorts of manure, you can imagine
the dead themselves, their boots, clothes and possessions
clinging to the ground, a man with no head
has a packet of chocolate and a souvenir of Tripoli.

[El Ballah, General Hospital, ? February 1943]

THE TRUMPET

O how often Arcturus
have you and your companions
heard the laughter and the distant shout
of the long tube a man sets to his mouth
crying that war is sweet, and the men you
see sleep after fighting will fight in the day before us?

Since with manual skill
men dressed to kill in purple
with how many strange tongues
cried the trumpet, that cried once
for the death of Hector from Troy steeple
that cried when a hundred hopes fell.

Tonight we heard it
who for weeks have only listened
to the howls of inhuman voices.
But as the apprehensive ear rejoiced,
breathing the notes in, the sky glistened
with a flight of bullets. We must be up early

tomorrow, to forget the cry and the crier
as we forgot the conversation
of our friends killed last month, last week
and hear, crouching, the air shriek
the crescendo, expectancy to elation
violently arriving. The trumpet is a liar.

[? El Ballah, General Hospital, 1943]

GALLANTRY

The Colonel in a casual voice
spoke into the microphone a joke
which through a hundred earphones broke
into the ears of a doomed race.

Into the ears of the doomed boy, the fool
whose perfectly mannered flesh fell
in opening the door for a shell
as he had learnt to do at school.

Conrad luckily survived the winter:
he wrote a letter to welcome
the auspicious spring: only his silken
intentions severed with a single splinter.

Was George fond of little boys?
We always suspected it,
but who will say: since George was hit
we never mention our surmise.

It was a brave thing the Colonel said,
but the whole sky turned too hot
and the three heroes never heard what
it was, gone deaf with steel and lead.

But the bullets cried with laughter,
the shells were overcome with mirth,
plunging their heads in steel and earth—
(the air commented in a whisper).

El Ballah, General Hospital, 1943

SNAKESKIN AND STONE

I praise a snakeskin or a stone:
a bald head and a public speech
I hate: the serpent's lozenges
are calligraphy, and it is
the truth these cryptograms teach
the pebble is truth alone.

Complication is belonging to the snake
who is as subtle as his gold, black, green
and it is right the stone is old
and smooth, utterly cruel and old.
These two are two pillars. Between
stand all the buildings truth can make,

a whole city, inhabited by lovers
murderers, workmen and artists
not much recognized: all
who have no memorial
but are mere men. Even the lowest
never made himself a mask of words or figures.

The bald head is a desert
between country of life and country of death
between the desolate projecting ears
move the wicked explorers, the flies
who know the dead bone is beneath
and from the skin the life half out.

The words are dying in heaps
in the papers they lie in rows
awaiting burial. The speaker's mouth
like a cold sea that sucks and spews them out
with insult to their bodies. Tangled they cruise
like mariners' bodies in the grave of ships.

Borrow hair for the bald crown
borrow applause for the dead words
for you who think the desert hidden
or the words, like the dry bones, living
are fit to profit from the world.
God help the lover of snakeskin and stone.

[? El Ballah, General Hospital, 1943]

WORDS

Words are my instruments but not my servants;
by the white pillar of a prince I lie in wait
for them. In what the hour or the minute invents,
in a web formally meshed or inchoate,
these fritillaries are come upon, trapped:
hot-coloured, or the cold scarabs a thousand years
old, found in cerements and unwrapped.
The catch and the ways of catching are diverse.
For instance this stooping man, the bones of whose face are
like the hollow birds' bones, is a trap for words.
And the pockmarked house bleached by the glare
whose insides war has dried out like gourds
attracts words. There are those who capture them
in hundreds, keep them prisoners in black
bottles, release them at exercise and clap them back.
But I keep words only a breath of time
turning in the lightest of cages—uncover
and let them go: sometimes they escape for ever.

El Ballah [General Hospital] 1943

107

DESERT FLOWERS

Living in a wide landscape are the flowers—
Rosenberg I only repeat what you were saying—
the shell and the hawk every hour
are slaying men and jerboas, slaying

the mind: but the body can fill
the hungry flowers and the dogs who cry words
at nights, the most hostile things of all.
But that is not new. Each time the night discards

draperies on the eyes and leaves the mind awake
I look each side of the door of sleep
for the little coin it will take
to buy the secret I shall not keep.

I see men as trees suffering
or confound the detail and the horizon.
Lay the coin on my tongue and I will sing
of what the others never set eyes on.

[? El Ballah, General Hospital, 1943]

LANDSCAPE WITH FIGURES 1*

Perched on a great fall of air
a pilot or angel looking down
on some eccentric chart, the plain
dotted with the useless furniture
discerns crouching on the sand vehicles
squashed dead or still entire, stunned
like beetles: scattered wingcases and
legs, heads, show when the haze settles.
But you who like Thomas come
to poke fingers in the wounds
find monuments, and metal posies:
on each disordered tomb
the steel is torn into fronds
by the lunatic explosive.

[? Tel Aviv, April 1943]

* In some versions, with the following two poems as a single
poem in three parts; see note, p. 155.

LANDSCAPE WITH FIGURES 2

On scrub and sand the dead men wriggle
in their dowdy clothes. They are mimes
who express silence and futile aims
enacting this prone and motionless struggle
at a queer angle to the scenery
crawling on the boards of the stage like walls
deaf to the one who opens his mouth and calls
silently. The décor is terrible tracery
of iron. The eye and mouth of each figure
bear the cosmetic blood and hectic
colours death has the only list of.
A yard more, and my little finger
could trace the maquillage of these stony actors
I am the figure writhing on the backcloth.

[? Tel Aviv, April 1943]

LANDSCAPE WITH FIGURES 3

I am the figure burning in hell
and the figure of the grave priest
observing everyone who passed
and that of the lover. I am all
the aimless pilgrims, the pedants and courtiers
more easily you believe me a pioneer
and a murdering villain without fear
without remorse hacking at the throat. Yes
I am all these and I am the craven
the remorseful the distressed
penitent: not passing from life to life
but all these angels and devils are driven
into my mind like beasts. I am possessed,
the house whose wall contains the dark strife
the arguments of hell with heaven.

[? April–September 1943]

SATURDAY EVENING IN
JERUSALEM*

In summer evenings Jerusalem fills
with movement of people, tides of speech
and the whole evening moving where
the words stream down into the square;
the street is full of shoulders. Watch
moonlight leap out between the hotels.

Young men and girls linked in fours or twos
under the moon sitting high and bright
are drawn uphill between the figures of trees
now softening the hot walls appear to freeze
and silver children to go in and out
stumping on the pavements with their shoes.

It is a collaboration between things
and people; the cat moonlight prowling about
rubs against friendly legs, leaps upon
the shoulders of a family. Family song,
incense of talk or laughter mounting the night;
in the dome of stars the moon sings.

But among these Jews I am the Jew
outcast, wandering down the steep road
into the hostile dark square:
and standing in the unlit corner here
know I am alone and cursed by God
like the boy lost on his first morning at school.

[? 1942–1944]

---

* For the relationship between this poem, 'Tel Aviv', and
'Jerusalem', see note, p. 155–6.

TEL AVIV

Like Ophelia in a lake of shadow lies
your face, a whiteness that draws down my lips
our hands meet like strangers in a city
among the glasses on the table tops
impervious to envy or pity
we whose drug is a meeting of the eyes.

In your locked mind your news from Russia is
and if I think, there is waiting Libya,
Tripoli, the many heads of war
are watching us. We are not unaware
but are this evening finding heavier
than war the scents of youth, youth's subtleties.

We who can't put out a single hand
to help our balance, who can never lean
on an old building in the past
or a new building in the future, must
balance tiptoe on a pin,
could teach an angel how to stand.

Do not laugh because I made a poem
it is to use what then we couldn't handle—
words of which we know the explosive
or poisonous tendency when we are too close. If
I had said this to you then, BANG will
have gone our walls of indifference in flame.

[? April 1943–1944]

JERUSALEM

Tonight there is a movement of things
the cat moonlight leaps out
between the dark hotels upon
the river of people; is gone
and in the dark words fall about.
In the dome of stars the moon sings.

Ophelia, in a pool of shadow lies
your face, flower that draws down my lips
our hands meet like strangers in a city
among the glasses on the table-top
impervious to envy or pity
we two lost in the country of our eyes.

We two, and other twos.
Stalingrad, Pacific, Tunis,
Tripoli, the many heads of war
are watching us. But now, and here
is night's short forgiveness
that all lovers use.

Now the dark theatre of the sky
encloses the conversation of the whole city
islanded, we sit under
the vault of it, and wonder
to hear such music in the petty
laughter and talk of passers-by.

[? 1944]

FRAGMENT

A

As at a final dance, I watch like two
to fix their picture—they are strange as gypsies
and turn invisible each minute,
the noble lunatics whose fancy is
that they are living still. Lord what a grace
their nonsense has, their pitiful delusion
that they like gentlemen agreed with Time.
Time who behind their backs turned them to smoke.
Listen, it is just possible to hear
the frail leaves of conversation falling
from the lips of a dead nobleman or king
while we remember what nobles and kings were.

B

As I watch each closely—for they are ghosts
and grow invisible before our eyes
I feel the hand of pity on my heart
shaken by their fealty to the past. Look,
their gestures. These in their rich lifetime bore
the mark of their nobility and pride.
Can you apparell in their proper gear
these skeletons of conversation falling
from the lips of a dead nobleman or a king
while still we know what nobles and kings were.

[? Tel Aviv, April 1943]

ENFIDAVILLE

In the church fallen like dancers
lie the Virgin and St Thérèse
on little pillows of dust.
The detonations of the last few days
tore down the ornamental plasters
shivered the hands of Christ.

The men and women who moved like candles
in and out of the houses and the streets
are all gone. The white houses are bare
black cages. No one is left to greet
the ghosts tugging at doorhandles
opening doors that are not there.

Now the daylight coming in from the fields
like a labourer, tired and sad,
is peering about among the wreckage, goes
past some corners as though with averted head
not looking at the pain this town holds,
seeing no one move behind the windows.

But already they are coming back; to search
like ants, poking in the débris, finding in it
a bed or a piano and carrying it out.
Who would not love them at this minute?
I seem again to meet
the blue eyes of the images in the church.

[? Tunisia, May 1943]

ARISTOCRATS*

The noble horse with courage in his eye,
clean in the bone, looks up at a shellburst:
away fly the images of the shires
but he puts the pipe back in his mouth.

Peter was unfortunately killed by an 88;
it took his leg away, he died in the ambulance.
I saw him crawling on the sand, he said
It's most unfair, they've shot my foot off.

How can I live among this gentle
obsolescent breed of heroes, and not weep?
Unicorns, almost,
for they are fading into two legends
in which their stupidity and chivalry
are celebrated. Each, fool and hero, will be an immortal.

These plains were their cricket pitch
and in the mountains the tremendous drop fences
brought down some of the runners. Here then
under the stones and earth they dispose themselves,
I think with their famous unconcern.
It is not gunfire I hear, but a hunting horn.

Tunisia 1943

* For another version, 'Sportsmen', see note, pp. 156–7.

VERGISSMEINNICHT*

Three weeks gone and the combatants gone
returning over the nightmare ground
we found the place again, and found
the soldier sprawling in the sun.

The frowning barrel of his gun
overshadowing. As we came on
that day, he hit my tank with one
like the entry of a demon.

Look. Here in the gunpit spoil
the dishonoured picture of his girl
who has put: *Steffi. Vergissmeinnicht*
in a copybook gothic script.

We see him almost with content,
abased, and seeming to have paid
and mocked at by his own equipment
that's hard and good when he's decayed.

But she would weep to see today
how on his skin the swart flies move;
the dust upon the paper eye
and the burst stomach like a cave.

For here the lover and killer are mingled
who had one body and one heart.
And death who had the soldier singled
has done the lover mortal hurt.

Tunisia [May–June] 1943

---

* For another version, 'The Lover', see note, p. 157–8.

HOW TO KILL

Under the parabola of a ball,
a child turning into a man,
I looked into the air too long.
The ball fell in my hand, it sang
in the closed fist: *Open Open*
Behold a gift designed to kill.

Now in my dial of glass appears
the soldier who is going to die.
He smiles, and moves about in ways
his mother knows, habits of his.
The wires touch his face: I cry
NOW. Death, like a familiar, hears

and look, has made a man of dust
of a man of flesh. This sorcery
I do. Being damned, I am amused
to see the centre of love diffused
and the waves of love travel into vacancy.
How easy it is to make a ghost.

The weightless mosquito touches
her tiny shadow on the stone,
and with how like, how infinite
a lightness, man and shadow meet.
They fuse. A shadow is a man
when the mosquito death approaches.

[? Tunisia–Cairo, 1943]

THIS IS THE DREAM*

The shadows of leaves falling like minutes.
Seascapes. Discoveries of sea creatures
and voices, out of the extreme distance, reach us
like conjured sounds.   Faces that are spirits,

cruise across the backward glance of the brain.
In the bowl of the mind is pot pourri.
Such shapes and hues become a lurid
décor to The Adventures. These are a cycle. When

I play dancer's choreographer's critic's role
I see myself dance happiness and pain
(each as illusory as rain)
in silence. Silence.   Break it with the small

tinkle;   apathetic buzz buzz
pirouetting into a crescendo, BANG.   Until
as each scene closes hush the stage is still,
everything is where it was.

The finale if it should come is

the moment my love and I meet
our hands move out across a room of strangers
certain they hold the rose of love.

[? Cairo, October 1943]

* For another version, 'I Experiment', see note, p. 159.

BEHAVIOUR OF FISH IN AN
EGYPTIAN TEA GARDEN

As a white stone draws down the fish
she on the seafloor of the afternoon
draws down men's glances and their cruel wish
for love. Slyly her red lip on the spoon

slips-in a morsel of ice-cream; her hands
white as a milky stone, white submarine
fronds, sink with spread fingers, lean
along the table, carmined at the ends.

A cotton magnate, an important fish
with great eyepouches and a golden mouth
through the frail reefs of furniture swims out
and idling, suspended, stays to watch.

A crustacean old man clamped to his chair
sits coldly near her and might see
her charms through fissures where the eyes should be
or else his teeth are parted in a stare.

Captain on leave, a lean dark mackerel
lies in the offing, turns himself and looks
through currents of sound. The flat-eyed flatfish sucks
on a straw, staring from its repose, laxly.

And gallants in shoals swim up and lag,
circling and passing near the white attraction;
sometimes pausing, opening a conversation:
fish pause so to nibble or tug.

Now the ice-cream is finished, is
paid for. The fish swim off on business:
and she sits alone at the table, a white stone
useless except to a collector, a rich man.

Cairo [? October] 1943

ENGLAND 1944

ACTORS WAITING IN THE WINGS OF EUROPE*

Actors waiting in the wings of Europe
we already watch the lights on the stage
and listen to the colossal overture begin.
For us entering at the height of the din
it will be hard to hear our thoughts, hard to gauge
how much our conduct owes to fear or fury.

Everyone, I suppose, will use these minutes
to look back, to hear music and recall
what we were doing and saying that year
during our last few months as people, near
the sucking mouth of the day that swallowed us all
into the stomach of a war. Now we are in it

and no more people, just little pieces of food
swirling in an uncomfortable digestive journey,
what we said and did then has a slightly
fairytale quality. There is an excitement
in seeing our ghosts wandering

[? March 1944]

---

* The final stanza of this poem is incomplete; see note, p. 160.

THE '*BÊTE NOIRE*' FRAGMENTS*

A (i)

Yes, I too have a particular monster
a toad or worm curled in the belly
stirring, eating at times I cannot foretell, he
is the thing I can admit only once to
anyone, never to those who have not their own.
Never to those who are happy, whose easy language
I speak well, though with a stranger's accent.

A (ii)

This is my particular monster. I know him;
he walks about inside me: I'm his house
and his landlord. He's my evacuee
taking a respite from hell in me
he decorates his room of course
to remind him of home. He often talks of going—

such a persuasive gentleman he is
I believe him, I go out quite sure
that I'll come back and find him gone
but does he go? Not him. No, he's a one
who likes his joke, he won't sit waiting for
me to come home, but comes

* The latest drafts of Douglas's various approaches to this poem; see
following 'Note on Drawing for the Jacket of *Bête Noire*'.

B

The Beast is a jailer
allows me out on parole
brings me back by telepathy
is inside my mind
breaks into my conversation with his own words,
speaking out of my mouth
can overthrow me in a moment
writes what I write, or edits it (censors it)
takes a dislike to my friends and sets me against them
can take away pleasure
is absent for long periods, is never expected when he returns
has several forms and disguises
makes enemies for me
can be overthrown by me, if I have help.
I have been trying to get help for about eleven years.
Three times I got help.
If this is a game, it's past half time and the beast is winning.

C

The trumpet man to take it away
blows a hot break in a beautiful way
ought to snap my fingers and tap my toes
but I sit at my table and nobody knows
I've got a beast on my back.

A medieval animal with a dog's face
Notre Dame or Chartres is his proper place
but here he is in the Piccadilly
sneering at the hot musicians' skill. He
is the beast on my back.

Suppose we dance, suppose we run away
into the street, or the underground
he'd come with us. It's his day.
Don't kiss me. Don't put your arm round
and touch the beast on my back

D

If at times my eyes are lenses
through which the brain explores
constellations of feeling
my ears yielding like swinging doors
admit princes to the corridors
into the mind, do not envy me.
I have a beast on my back

[February–March 1944]

Note on Drawing for the Jacket of *Bête Noire*

Bête Noire is the name of the poem I can't write; a protracted failure, which is also a protracted success I suppose. Because it is the poem I begin to write in a lot of other poems: this is what justifies my use of that title for the book. The beast, which I have drawn as black care sitting behind the horseman, is indefinable: sitting down to try and describe it, I have sensations of physical combat, and after five hours of writing last night, which resulted in failure, all my muscles were tired. But if he is not caught, at least I can see his tracks (anyone may see them), in some of the other poems. My failure is that I know so little about him, beyond his existence and the infinite patience and extent of his malignity. Examining what I do know, I write down:

> He is a jailer.
> Allows me out on parole
> brings me back by telepathy
> is inside my mind
> breaks into my conversation with his own words
> speaking out of my mouth
> can overthrow me in a moment
> can be overthrown, if I have help
> writes with my hand, and censors what I write
> takes a dislike to my friends and sets me against them
> can take away pleasure
> is absent for long periods, shows up without notice
> employs disguise.
> If this is a game, it's past half-time and the beast is winning.

This isn't much help. Nor is the suggestion that he is

> a medieval animal with a dog's face
> Notre Dame or Chartres is his proper place.

I am afraid I know nothing about this beast at all: he is so amorphous and powerful that he could be a deity. Only he is implacable; no use sacrificing to him, he takes what he wants.

> Yes, I too have a particular monster
> a toad or worm curled in the belly
> stirring, eating at times I cannot tell, he
> is the thing I can admit only once to
> anyone, never to those who have not their own,
> never to those who are happy.

The quotations of course are from my own failures to write 'Bête Noire'.

[March 1944]

TO KRISTIN YINGCHENG
OLGA MILENA

Women of four countries
the four phials full of essences
of green England, legendary China,
cold Europe, Arabic Spain, a finer
four poisons for the subtle senses
than any in medieval inventories.

Here I give back perforce
the sweet wine to the grape
give the dark plant its juices
what every creature uses
by natural law will seep
back to the natural source.

[? March 1944]

ON A RETURN FROM EGYPT

To stand here in the wings of Europe
disheartened, I have come away
from the sick land where in the sun lay
the gentle sloe-eyed murderers
of themselves, exquisites under a curse;
here to exercise my depleted fury.

For the heart is a coal, growing colder
when jewelled cerulean seas change
into grey rocks, grey water-fringe,
sea and sky altering like a cloth
till colour and sheen are gone both:
cold is an opiate of the soldier.

And all my endeavours are unlucky explorers
come back, abandoning the expedition;
the specimens, the lilies of ambition
still spring in their climate, still unpicked:
but time, time is all I lacked
to find them, as the great collectors before me.

The next month, then, is a window
and with a crash I'll split the glass.
Behind it stands one I must kiss,
person of love or death
a person or a wraith,
I fear what I shall find.

[? March–April 1944]

TWO STATEMENTS ON POETRY

1. Oxford 1940

Poetry is like a man, whom thinking you know all his movements and appearance you will presently come upon in such a posture that for a moment you can hardly believe it a position of the limbs you know. So thinking you have set bounds to the nature of poetry, you shall as soon discover something outside your bounds which they should evidently contain.

The expression 'bad poetry' is meaningless: critics still use it, forgetting that bad poetry is not poetry at all.

Nor can prose and poetry be compared any more than pictures and pencils: the one is instrument and the other art. Poetry may be written in prose or verse, or spoken extempore.

For it is anything expressed in words, which appeals to the emotions either in presenting an image or picture to move them; or by the music of words affecting them through the senses; or in stating some truth whose eternal quality exacts the same reverence as eternity itself.

In its nature poetry is sincere and simple.

Writing which is poetry must say what the writer has himself to say, not what he has observed others to say with effect, nor what he thinks will impress his hearers because it impressed him hearing it. Nor must he waste any more words over it than a mathematician: every word must work for its keep, in prose, blank verse, or rhyme.

And poetry is to be judged not by what the poet has tried to say; only by what he has said.

(Douglas's contribution to a symposium 'On the Nature of Poetry', published in *Augury: An Oxford Miscellany of Verse and Prose*, 1940)

2. Palestine 1943

. . . Incidentally you say I fail as a poet, when you mean I fail as a lyricist. Only someone who is out of touch, by which I mean first hand touch, with what has happened outside England—and from a cultural point of view I wish it had affected English life more—could make that criticism. I am surprised you should still expect me to produce musical verse. A lyric form and a lyric approach will do even less good than a journalese approach to the subjects we have to discuss now. I don't know if you have come across the word Bullshit—it is an army word and signifies humbug and unnecessary detail. It symbolizes what I think must be got rid of—the mass of irrelevancies, of 'attitudes', 'approaches', propaganda, ivory towers, etc., that stands between us and our problems and what we have to do about them.

To write on the themes which have been concerning me lately in lyrical and abstract forms, would be immense bullshitting. In my early poems I wrote lyrically, as an innocent, because I was an innocent: I have (not surprisingly) fallen from that particular grace since then. I had begun to change during my second year at Oxford. T. S. Eliot wrote to me when I first joined the army, that I appeared to have finished with one form of writing and to be progressing towards another, which he did not think I had mastered. I knew this to be true, without his saying it. Well, I am still changing: I don't disagree with you if you say I am awkward and not used to the new paces yet. But my object (and I don't give a damn about my duty as a poet) is to write true things, significant things in words each of which works for its place in a line. My rhythms, which you find enervated, are carefully chosen to enable the poems to be *read* as significant speech: I see no reason to be either musical or sonorous about things at present. When I do, I shall be so again, and glad to. I suppose I reflect the cynicism and the careful absence of expectation (it is not quite the same as apathy) with which I view the world. As many others to whom I have spoken, not only civilians and British soldiers, but German and Italians, are in the same state of mind, it is a true reflection. I never tried to write about war (that is battles and things, not London can Take it), with the exception of a satiric picture of some soldiers frozen to death, until I had experienced it. Now I will write of it, and perhaps one day cynic and lyric will meet and make me a balanced style. Certainly you will never see the long metrical similes and galleries of images again.

Your talk of regrouping sounds to me—if you will excuse me for exhibiting a one-track mind—like the military excuse of a defeated general. There is never much need to regroup. Let your impulses drive you forward; never lose contact with life or you will lose the impulses as well. Meanwhile if you must regroup, do it by re-reading your old stuff.

Of course, you will never take my advice nor I yours. But in these tirades a few ideas do scrape through the defences on either side. Perhaps all this may make it easier for you to understand why I am writing the way I am and why I shall never go back to the old forms. You may even begin to see some virtue in it. To be sentimental or emotional now is dangerous to oneself and to others. To trust anyone or to admit any hope of a better world is criminally foolish, as foolish as it is to stop working for it. It sounds silly to say work without hope, but it can be done; it's only a form of insurance; it doesn't mean work hopelessly.

(From a letter on airgraphs Douglas wrote to J. C. Hall, 10 August 1943. Reprinted from earlier collections; one of the airgraphs remains in Hall's possession; the others have been lost.)

NOTES

NOTES

The notes which follow give the source for each poem printed, describe other texts where the variants are substantial, list the first publication of each poem, and give further information, textual and contextual, of particular interest. The reader may wish also to consult the biography of Douglas by the present editor, published in 1974 and frequently cited here, the detailed description of the Keith Douglas Papers in the British Library before 1972 in the volume *The Arts Council Collection of Modern Literary Manuscripts 1963–1972*, and *Keith Douglas: A Prose Miscellany* (1985), which contains both sides of Douglas's literary correspondance.

Manuscript sources, public and private, available to this editor up to 1973 are listed in the biography. A principal source for Douglas manuscript material is still the British Library, whose collection has been augmented since 1973. The Brotherton Library at the University of Leeds now holds virtually all Douglas's surviving personal library, his copies of periodicals, and miscellaneous papers several of which have drafts or notes referred to here. Since 1973 two further groups of manuscripts have been located: letters from Douglas to Edmund Blunden, including the texts of 11 poems, now in the Humanities Research Center at the University of Texas; and certain papers remaining with Douglas's first publishers, Editions Poetry London Ltd (other papers from the same source are in the Douglas Papers at the British Library), and later passed by Mrs Richard March to J. C. Hall. These last are now in the British Library (Add. MSS 60585-9) along with the MS cited below as Graham MS (Add. MS. 61938: a second exercise book is 61939).

Individuals frequently mentioned in the notes are Keith Douglas (KD), his mother, Mrs Marie J. Douglas (MJD), and Edmund Blunden, J. C. Hall, and M. J. Tambimuttu (referred to by surname only). 'KD's list (? Sept. 1943)', frequently cited, is a list of titles he drew up, probably in September 1943, in connection with the collection of his poems proposed by Tambimuttu; it is in the British Library (Add. MS. 53773, f. 45b). Other abbreviations and short forms used are given below. For published works, the place of publication is London unless otherwise noted.

PRINCIPAL SOURCES CITED

Books	*Cited as*

(i) by Keith Douglas:

Augury: An Oxford Miscellany of Verse and Prose, ed. K. C.
Douglas and A. M. Hardie (Oxford: Basil Blackwell,
1940)   *Augury*

Selected Poems, Keith Douglas, J. C. Hall and Norman
Nicholson, Modern Reading Library No.3 (John Bale and
Staples, 1943)   *SP* 1943

Alamein to Zem Zem [with an appendix of poems],   *Alamein*
Editions Poetry London (Nicholson and Watson, 1946)   1946

Collected Poems, ed. John Waller and G. S. Fraser, Editions
Poetry London (Nicholson and Watson, 1951)   *CP* 1951

Collected Poems, ed. John Waller, G. S. Fraser and J. C.
Hall (Faber and Faber, 1966)   *CP* 1966

(ii) on Keith Douglas:

Desmond Graham, *Keith Douglas 1920–1944: a biography*
(Oxford University Press, 1974)   *KD*

Jenny Stratford, *The Arts Council Collection of Modern
Literary Manuscripts 1963–1972* (Turret Books, 1974),
pp. 44–61, 118–30, where the Keith Douglas Papers in
the British Library are described: the relevant discussion
in this work has been cited when a poem first published
in *CP* 1951 has variants from the text printed here.   *S*

Periodicals

Cited in full in each instance, with the place of
publication when other than London, except for *The
Outlook* (Christ's Hospital, Horsham), *The Cherwell*
(Oxford), and *Citadel* and *Personal Landscape* (Cairo), cited
by title only.

Unpublished material

THE BRITISH LIBRARY
Keith Douglas Papers, cited by Add. MS. number and
folio   BL

BROTHERTON LIBRARY, UNIVERSITY OF LEEDS
(i) Books, periodicals, etc. from KD's library   Brotherton
                                                                                          Collection
(ii) Nine autograph copies of poems sent to Mary   Brotherton
     Benson, about September 1941   MS.

HUMANITIES RESEARCH CENTER, UNIVERSITY OF TEXAS
Letters and poems sent to Edmund Blunden   Texas MS.

IN PRIVATE HANDS IN 1978, AND NOW IN THE BRITISH LIBRARY
Editions Poetry London material in the possession of J. C. Hall
(i)   39 folio typescripts and 5 folio carbon typescripts
      from the collection KD prepared in 1940–1 and in
      part revised in 1943–4   EPL TS.
(ii) Other manuscripts in KD's hands in 1943–4 left
      with Editions Poetry London in 1944; cited in each
      case with a description of the manuscript or
      typescript   EPL MS.
(iii) Other papers in this collection, including autograph
      letters, typescripts made for posthumous editions
      of KD's work, and correspondence relating to these
      editions   EPL Papers

School exercise book in the possession of the present
editor, titled by KD 'Poems 1934–6' (referred to in the
biography as '1934–6')   Graham MS.

OTHER MANUSCRIPTS
In the possession of J. C. Hall, Alec Hardie, Mrs A. G.
Haysom, Mrs J. F. O'Neill, and Mrs Phyllis Thayer, cited
by the owner's surname only

SCHOOL
Mummers
EPL TS. Pub. *Outlook*, Dec. 1936, p. 18, as 'Mummers—a Christmas
Poem', with variants incl. ll. 17–18 '. . . and blade time-rusted / The fabled
Saint and Dragon fight.'

Youth
Outlook, Apr. 1936, p. 13; in Graham MS., 'Transitional Stage', with variants.

Strange Gardener
Outlook, Apr. 1936, p. 7; in Graham MS., 'Transitional Stage', with variants. An autograph copy in an exercise book of '24.1.36' (now BL 59834) is analysed by KD with notes on its allusions and echoes—of F. Prokosch, Henry Williamson, C. Day Lewis, T. S. Eliot, and *The Tempest*.

.303
Outlook, Apr. 1936, p. 12; in Graham MS., 'Transitional Stage', with variants.

Bexhill
EPL TS., with autograph note 'with a group of "Juvenilia" if at all. KCD'. In Graham MS., 'Later Style', with title 'Love and Gorizia' and two stanzas:

LOVE AND GORIZIA

And now in the South the swallows
swirling precisely among the dazzled trees
are not known, not at this season, among these
small streets and posters which the lamplight shews:
but are among the white-dusted avenues,
and where the ruined palace faces the green
river, and barbers chatter, the sky is clean.

Mr. Kennedy, speaking in Painswick among slate,
insisted on shadows' value, thought
colour of merely secondary import;
characteristically, being himself incomplete,
wound-drained, among these places, where thus late
the unsatisfied put out their heads, take pleasure
in reproducing rooftops on rough paper.

This my comparison of where I found you
with South, redolent of wingtips, suddenly gold,
you small with your red-brown hair how could I mould,
so inconsistent, how could I take you? So renew
desires, Birdlip for Aquileia, different view

> forswearing swallows. Spinsters on their stools
> more valuable than monks until Desire cools.

For KD's visit to Gorizia see *KD*, pp. 30–33.

Caravan
EPL TS., with comma l. 9 from *Programme* (Oxford), where pub. June 1937, p. 11, with variants.

Images
EPL TS., which has autograph note 'I don't like this much myself KCD'. Variant title in Graham MS.: 'The Eagle in Praise of Poets'. Pub. *Cherwell*, 18 May 1940.

Famous Men
EPL MS., red TS., which has autograph note (in response to Blunden's comment beside l. 7, 'I'm puzzled by this') 'Cut this out too if you like— it's only included as Juvenilia, date about 1934–5'. Variant title in Graham MS.: 'Epitaph'. Pub. *Cherwell*, 27 Apr. 1940, p. 8. An early draft with extensive variants is quoted and discussed in *KD*, pp. 42–3.

Distraction
EPL TS., where title is deleted: 'Classroom' inserted in pencil but probably not autograph. Pub. *Outlook*, Dec. 1936, p. 14, with title 'Distraction from Classics' and variants incl., after l. 7:

> We crouch to read the speech of other ages.

> Many were here, some cursed, loved some. All these
> Alike pass; after a space return,
> Loud-voiced, mocking the older memories.

Encounter with a God
EPL TS. Pub. *Outlook*, July 1936, p. 8, as 'Japanese Song', with variants. Variant title in *Cherwell*, 9 Mar. 1940, p. 123: 'Japanese'.

Dejection
EPL TS. Pub. *New Verse*, Mar. 1938, p. 8, with variants incl. an additional line between ll. 8 and 9: 'Shrieks through the mist and scatters the pools of stars.' and no italics. For KD and *New Verse*, see *KD*, pp. 41, 61.

A Storm
EPL TS., with autograph pencil title; 'Sonnet' deleted. Pub. *Bolero* (Oxford), Spring 1939, p. 8, as 'Sonnet', with variants.

Villanelle of Gorizia
EPL TS. Pub. *Outlook*, Dec. 1937, p. 7, with ll. 16–17 'All this the bottle says, that I have quite / Poured out. The wine slides in my throat and grieves.' and omitting the final line, added in autograph in KD's copy (Brotherton Collection).

Point of View
BL 53773, f. 2, autograph copy, the source for the uncorrected EPL TS. Pub. *Outlook*, Apr. 1938, p. 16, with variants incl. ll. 9–12:

> Yes, if this sort of thing is your middle name:
> Or if you are at home, sit and cry shame
> To step at the dusk's edge with seductive summer,
> Shut out the fields and search for facts too fast—

Kristin
EPL TS. Pub. *Outlook*, July 1938, p. 14, with variants incl. l. 15 'But look, bedewèd violets lip the rain,'. For Kristin, see *KD*, pp. 57 ff.

On Leaving School
EPL TS., which has autograph pencil note 'Might be worth incl. as Early poem'. Pub. *Outlook*, Apr. 1938, p. 13, as 'Sonnet', with variants.

Pleasures
EPL TS., with pencil change of 'forgotten' to 'forgot' in ll. 13 and 21; TS. has ink autograph note 'School age 18'. Variant title in Haysom MS.: 'Exotic'. Pub. *Bolero* (Oxford), Winter 1938, as 'Poem from a Sequence', with variants followed by *SP* 1943, where it has title 'Forgotten the Red Leaves'.

OXFORD

Spring Sailor
EPL TS. Pub. *Fords and Bridges* (Oxford), May 1939, p. 24, with variants.

Poor Mary
EPL TS. Pub. *Fords and Bridges* (Oxford), May 1939, p. 24, with variants.
For Mary, see *KD*, pp. 72–3.

Stranger
EPL TS., with date from red TS. (BL 56357, f. 22). Pub. *Cherwell*, 9 Mar.
1940, p. 124, with variants; dedication from there. For a variant autograph
copy sent to 'Y[ing] C[heng] S[ze]', and its accompanying letter, see *KD*,
pp. 71–3.

Invaders
EPL TS., with autograph revisions. Pub. *Oxford Magazine*, 26 Oct. 1939,
p. 28, with variants.

Pas de Trois
Brotherton MS., with punctuation from *Augury*. Pub. *Oxford Magazine*, 9
Nov. 1939, p. 57, with variants, incl. additional line at beginning of final
stanza: 'Today when smartness does for grace'.

Do not look up
Haysom MS., autograph copy ? Dec. 1939 (see *KD*, p. 91). Pub. 1978 ed.,
previously unpub.

Stars
BL 56357, f. 27, carbon TS. Pub. *Oxford Magazine*, 30 Nov. 1939, p. 109,
with title 'Addison and I', no dedication, the epigraph 'What though in
solemn silence all / Move round the dark terrestrial ball?', and variants,
incl. a fourth stanza:

> On Earth, who stands attendant in his place
> Among that regiment, we walk. And still,
> Though all whom woman ever brought to birth
> Are not a shadow on the face of Earth,
> We feel companionship, and the goodwill
> Between us and that strange removed race.

Dedication from *SP* 1943. For Antoinette, see *KD*, pp. 81 ff.

Haydn—Military Symphony
BL 56357, f. 25, carbon TS. Pub. *Augury*, p. 26.

Haydn—Clock Symphony
EPL TS. Pub. *Kingdom Come* (Oxford), Dec. 1939–Jan. 1940, p. 43, with a fourth stanza:

> Yet you Death's servant must return to service:
> Re-enter the hall and find the solemn clock
> Who cries that Time's alive. And so put on
> Your garment of sad days and get you gone.
> Against you and your raucous world they'll lock,
> But open up when you forsake Death's service.

Variant title in Haysom MS.: 'A Symphony of Haydn'.

To a Lady on the Death of Her First Love
Cherwell, 27 Apr. 1940, p. 8; also an autograph copy (O'Neill MS.). Previously uncollected.

Sanctuary
EPL TS. Pub. *Cherwell*, 3 Feb. 1940, p. 45, with variants.

The Creator
EPL MS., red TS., with autograph pencil revisions and Blunden note: 'I wonder if this is up to the standard of fresh Idea through the poems' and KD's autograph rejoinder: 'Yes, Cut this if you like'. Pub. *Cherwell*, 2 Mar. 1940, p. 97, with variants.

Villanelle of Sunlight
Cherwell, 9 Mar. 1940, p. 123, where pub. under pseudonym 'Tancred Paul'. No known MS.

Gender Rhyme
EPL TS., carbon. Pub. *Cherwell*, 9 Mar. 1940, p. 122, with variants.

Russians
BL 53773, f. 10, autograph copy ?1944; punctuation from EPL TS., which has variants. Pub. *Kingdom Come* (Oxford), Spring 1940, p. 71, with variants. KD noted on a MS. sent to Olga Meiersens (BL 53773, f. 11): 'During the Russian campaign against Finland, a Russian regiment was reported to have been discovered frozen to death, the soldiers still holding their rifles ready to fire.'

Farewell Poem
EPL TS., with autograph revisions; TS. has autograph note 'omit'. Pub. *Cherwell*, 27 Apr. 1940, p. 16, with variants.

Villanelle of Spring Bells
BL 56357, f. 5, autograph MS. in a letter (? 1942) with 'Song: Dotards . . .', but correcting final line 'ancient' for 'aged'. Pub. *Augury*, p. 23, with variants: colon l. 14 followed here.

Canoe
Cherwell, 18 May 1940 where ll. 2–3 read 'a part / of pleasure', presumably in error. No known MS.

A Round Number
BL 56357, f. 30, carbon TS., where it is part II of 'Despair', with part I:

> Are you fair now? It is no matter,
> day will as sure as stone discover
> your elegance and beauty over.
> Foul as a yellow ferret
> you who were the rose the fragrance linger
>
> who were the rose a royal
> bloom of polite love, oh how you change
> flower to animal; and now impinge
> where once you sanctified with sweet merit,
> which evil experience can spoil.
>
> But I am yours and must
> lie in the very bog where I am anchored
> as low as you, as coarse and cankered,
> fallen to lie with humming lust.
>
> God knows how we shall get again
> the drug of love and the sweet pain.

Pub. as 'A Round Number', *Cherwell*, 25 May 1940, p. 76, with variants. An illustration for *Bête Noire* (reproduced *CP* 1966, p. 60) made in 1944 has title 'A Round Number'.

A God is Buried
BL 56357, ff. 31–2, carbon TS. but text of part I following later MS. (BL

53773, f. 7), part IV Brotherton MS. (where it has title 'The God Speaks'). Part I pub. as 'Search for a God', *Kingdom Come* (Oxford), Summer 1940, p. 134, with variants; parts II–IV unpub. KD included 'Burial of a God' in a list of suggestions for *SP* 1943, with the note 'part 1 in Kingdom Come, the rest unpublished' (airletter to Hall [17 Oct. 1941], BL 53773, f. 43). The original TS. of the poem in four parts is missing from EPL TS., as confirmed by letter from Richard March to MJD 21 June 1949 (EPL Papers); there is a fragmentary MS. of part I (? 1944; BL 53773, f. 6).

Shadows
EPL TS. Pub. *Cherwell*, 15 June 1940, p. 118, with variants.

A Mime
EPL MS., red TS., with autograph revisions in ink and pencil; dash l. 4 from *Cherwell*, where pub. 15 June 1940, p. 118, with variants.

The Deceased
EPL MS., red TS., with autograph revisions; final couplet (deleted): 'Respect him, for in this / he had an excellence you miss.' TS. has space between couplets, bracketed with autograph pencil note 'Print all together'. Pub. *Cherwell*, 15 June 1940, p. 118 (in couplets), with variants.

Soissons
Cherwell, 15 June 1940, p. 118. EPL red TS. has Blunden note: 'I don't think this a lucky ending . . .', and autograph ink revision to final sentence. KD's copy of *SP* 1943 (Brotherton Collection) has an autograph translation into French of stanzas 1 and 2. For KD's visit to Soissons with Hamo Sassoon in March/April 1939, see *KD*, pp. 74–5.

Soissons 1940
EPL TS. Pub. *SP* 1943, p. 13.

Absence
EPL red TS., with italics from Hardie MS. which has title 'The Garden' and variants. Pub. *Poetry (London)*, Sept. 1949, p. 4, with title 'Absence'.

The Poets
BL 56357, f. 37, carbon TS. Pub. *CP* 1951, p. 101, a text apparently conflated from MSS. (see *S*, p. 48).

To Curse Her
EPL TS., with autograph revisions and title; 'Reproach' deleted. Pub. *CP* 1951, p. 79 (without autograph revisions). An earlier draft (BL 53773, f. 13b) was written at the same stage as 'The Poets' (see above).

A Ballet
EPL TS. Hardie MS. has variants. Pub. *CP* 1951, p. 87.

An Oration
BL 56357, f. 42, carbon TS., with autograph revisions; autograph revision to EPL TS. is incomplete. Pub. *CP* 1951, p. 93, with variants (see *S*, pp. 49, 127–8).

Leukothea
EPL TS. Hardie MS. has title 'Leukothea' deleted and replaced by 'A speech for an Actor'; stanza breaks at ll. 4, 10, 14; and variants including final lines: 'O hell and Fury then, my trust's betrayed / what are these bones, bones, bones so disarrayed?' Pub. *Poetry Scotland* (Glasgow), July 1946, p. 39, with title 'Leukothea' and further variants.

John Anderson
EPL TS. Hardie MS. has variant punctuation; for KD's request for 'the stuff in inverted commas in italics' (lacking in EPL TS.) and for an early draft, see *KD*, pp. 101–2 and 270. Pub. *Poetry (London)*, Sept.–Oct. 1947, p. 10 (as EPL TS.).

FOUR TRANSLATIONS

Horace: Odes I:v: EPL TS., but following autograph revisions to Haysom MS. Pub. *Cherwell*, 9 Mar. 1940, p. 124, with variants.

Le Dormeur du Val: Cherwell, 27 Apr. 1940, p. 13; unsigned. No known MS.

Au Cabaret-Vert: Cherwell, 4 May 1940, p. 17; signed 'K'. No known MS.

Head of a Faun: EPL TS., but following l. 2 'all' deleted by KD on leaf from *Eight Oxford Poets* (Brotherton Collection), which also carries autograph date. Pub. *Cherwell*, 4 May 1940, p. 32.

ARMY: ENGLAND

An Exercise Against Impatience
EPL TS., but following BL 56357, f. 3, l. 2 'fall' for 'fell'. TS. has additional stanza at end, deleted in pencil:

> and without prophets, what is there
> in the crucible, the inscrutable cavern
> and what all the signs have given
> you can be certain, will appear.

This is followed by an autograph pencil fragment, also deleted: 'And when this canned incorporate society / is opened and consumed, then who can doubt / Time in digesting it will'. Pub. *CP* 1951, p. 89, in seven stanzas.

The News from Earth
EPL TS., which has autograph note 'unsatisfactory end' and a deleted sixth stanza:

> Yes, Jove shouts once, and the whole illusion
> chromium and machinery falls in fine confusion,
> vanishes like a trick with all who lived by it.
> Yet none of us could wonder at the sight
> of what might seem a wonderful conclusion.

Pub. *Platitude* (Oxford), vol. II, no. 10 (Hilary Term 1941), in six stanzas with variants.

Extension to Francis Thompson
Cherwell, 30 Jan. 1941, p. 28. No known MS. KD suggested the poem be included 'under a less pretentious title' in *SP* 1943 (airletter to Hall [17 Oct. 1941], BL 53773, f. 43).

The Prisoner
Citadel, Jan. 1943, p. 17; autograph date from EPL TS., which has variants: *SP* 1943 has ll. 5–7 'but mothwise my hands return / to your fair cheek as luminous as / a lamp . . .' and ll. 12–13 '. . . stone / person of death . . .'.

Oxford
EPL TS., with autograph title; 'The City' deleted. Pub. *CP* 1951, p. 96.

The House

EPL TS., with autograph revisions; TS. has autograph note 'Probably needs correction etc.' Pub. *Poetry (London)*, Nov.–Dec. 1948, p. 2. Autograph copy sent to T. S. Eliot (BL 53773, ff. 31–2) has marginal notes by Eliot (see *KD*, pp. 138–9, 273–4).

Time Eating

BL 53773, f. 35, autograph copy ?1944. KD gave a book (Thayer MS.) with an early draft on endpapers to his Wickwar landlady (see *KD*, p. 120). Pub. *Citadel*, Nov. 1942, p. 37, omitting ll. 11–14 (also omitted in Brotherton MS.), and with other variants. Autograph copy with notes by Eliot (BL 53773, f. 36) as for 'The House' (see above).

Song: Dotards . . .

Brotherton MS., but following EPL TS. punctuation and l. 7 'a' for 'and'; latter has autograph date. BL. 56357, f. 5, probably a later copy ?1942, is imperfect, but has variants incl. l. 5 'death' for 'Fate'. Pub. *CP* 1951, p. 55, with variants (as EPL TS.). Autograph copy with notes by Eliot (BL 53773, f. 40) as for 'The House' (see above).

The Marvel

BL 53773, f. 35b, autograph copy ?1944; autograph date from EPL TS., which has stanzas 5–7 bracketed, and note 'Omit?'. Brotherton MS. has date 'Merton College, Oxford' (? in error), and omits stanzas 5–7. An early draft (BL 53773, f. 37) has title 'The Monument'. Pub. *Cherwell*, 19 June 1941, p. 122, with variants. Autograph copy with notes by Eliot (BL 53773, f. 38) as for 'The House' (see above). For KD and Linney Head, see *KD*, p. 121.

Simplify me when I'm dead

BL 56357, f. 52, carbon TS. Pub. *Poetry (London)*, no. X (Dec. 1944). All MSS. untitled; title here from *CP* 1951, source unknown. A MS. draft is reproduced in *KD*, p. 127.

ARMY: MIDDLE EAST

Song: Do I venture . . .

EPL MS., TS. airgraph to MJD 12 Aug. [1942]. Date from an earlier copy in an airletter to Hall [17 Oct. 1941] (BL 53773, f. 43b), which has variants incl. fourth stanza:

> All day on a flat calm we steer
> but though the false sea fawn and curl
> for weeks it has not calmed me.
> Let them bind me to the rail
> for the poisonous sea and a cruel star
> the one by day and one at night have charmed me.

beside which KD noted 'I am in 2 minds, whether or not to include this verse'. Pub. *Poetry (London)*, Nov.–Dec. 1947, p. 4, with further variants.

The Two Virtues

Texas MS., in autograph airletter to Blunden [26 Oct. 1941]. Pub. 1978 ed.; previously unpub. KD's list (? Sept. 1943) has title 'Lovers 2 Virtues'.

Negative Information

BL 53773, f. 43b, in autograph airletter to Hall [17 Oct. 1941], but following *SP* 1943 for ll. 22–3 punctuation. Pub. *SP* 1943, p. 48.

The Hand

Citadel, Oct. 1942, p. 34. Date from an earlier variant MS. (BL 53773, f. 44).

Adams and The Sea Bird

Adams: Texas MS., in autograph airletter to Blunden [26 Oct. 1941]. Pub. *Poetry (London)*, June–July 1948, p. 19, with variants as EPL MS. (a TS. of unknown date).

The Sea Bird: Citadel, Jan. 1943, p. 16, dated in error 'Nathanya 1942'; no known MS. For a letter relating to this poem, see *KD*, pp. 132–3.

These grasses, ancient enemies and Syria

These grasses, ancient enemies: EPL MS., TS. airgraph to Hall 30 Nov. 1941; untitled, with note 'use the first line as a title'; also Texas MS. Pub. *Poetry Scotland* (Glasgow), July 1946, p. 40.

Syria: Citadel, July 1942, p. 23, but following EPL MS. (TS. copy in airgraph from Milena Gutierrez Pegna to MJD 9 Sept. 1942) l. 1 beginning 'These' for 'The'; comma l. 18 end added by ed. A rough autograph copy (BL 53773, f. 45) was made in ? 1943. For KD's visit to Syria in November 1941, see *KD*, pp. 139–40.

Egyptian Sentry, Corniche, Alexandria

BL 53773, f. 95, autograph copy 1944. Date from KD's stay in Alexandria (see *KD*, p. 274). Pub. *Alamein* 1946, p. xv.

L'Autobus

BL 53773, f. 93, autograph copy 1944. Date as for 'Egyptian Sentry . . .' (see above). Pub. *Alamein* 1946, p. xii.

Devils

T.L.S., 23 Jan. 1943, p. 46. An earlier text in an airgraph to MJD 18 Aug. 1942 (BL 56355, f. 138) has numerous variants; EPL MS. has slight variants.

Egypt

BL 56355, f. 139, in TS. airletter to MJD 20 Sept. 1942, also sending 'Christodoulos'. Pub. *Poetry (London)*, Nov.–Dec. 1948, p. 1.

Christodoulos

BL 56355, f. 139, in TS. airletter as for 'Egypt' (see above). Pub. *Alamein* 1946, p. v.

The Knife

EPL MS., in TS. airletter to MJD 18 Oct. 1942, with autograph revisions; colon l. 13 from Hall MS., which has dedication at foot 'For M[ilena] G[utierrez] P[egna]'. Pub. *Poetry (London)*, Nov.–Dec. 1947, p. 5. For KD and Milena, see *KD*, pp. 151–60.

I listen to the desert wind

EPL MS., untitled TS. with autograph revisions. An autograph copy (BL 53773, f. 47) has title 'Milena' and variants. KD's list (? Sept. 1943) has title 'Listen to Desert wind'. Pub. *Poetry (London)*, Nov.–Dec. 1948, p. 1.

The Offensive 1 and 2

The Offensive 1: EPL MS., TS. with title 'Moonlight, Wadi Natrun' and autograph note entering the poem in a competition. An autograph copy in a letter to Olga Meiersens ? 25 Jan. 1943 (BL 56357, f. 7) has title 'Lines written before the Alamein offensive'.

The Offensive 2: BL 53773, f. 48, in airgraph to MJD 10 Jan. 1943; untitled.

'Offensive 1' and 'Offensive 2' are given as two poems in KD's list (?

Sept. 1943). Both poems pub. *Citadel*, Feb. 1943, p. 16, as a single poem with title 'Reflections of the New Moon in Sand', in two parts and with variants close to earlier Hall MS. and EPL MS. (both in TS. airletters of 18 Oct. 1942 with title 'The Offensive'). In all these versions 'The Offensive 2' lacks final stanza and begins 'The stars dead heroes in the sky'.

Mersa

BL 53773, f. 49, autograph copy 1944; KD notes in accompanying letter to Betty Jesse (EPL Papers), 'Will you look up SKELETAL in a dictionary (I haven't one) and find out if it exists and means like a skeleton. If not alter skeletal in MERSA to skeleton.' Pub. *Alamein* 1946, p. x, with variants (source unknown) incl. l. 9 'ruined hive of a' for 'skeletal'. For KD at Mersa, see *KD*, pp. 171–4.

Dead Men

Citadel, Mar. 1943, p. 24, with autograph corrections from KD's copy (Brotherton Collection): commas added ll. 11 and 20, l. 13 moved to stanza 3. No known MS.

Cairo Jag

Personal Landscape, vol. II, no. 2 (? Summer 1944), p. 11. An autograph copy in a letter to Olga Meiersens ? Feb. 1943 (BL 53773, ff. 57–57b) is in four sections (the second beginning at 'But by a day's travelling . . .'), with slight variants, and continues:

> III
>
> There are new ethics here and fresh virtues.
> We have our wise men and lawgivers
> artists—for we discovered new arts:
> I think some have new religions, and
> there are socialites, the smart set, rulers
> and little rulers. In all this dry land
> the beautiful trees of metal
> the noble dead whom we honour as companions
> with every indignity, the music is loud or soft
> as variable and unexpected as the swing bands
> as the classical orchestra of Sculz in Cairo.

IV

You do not gradually appreciate such qualities
but your mind will extend new hands. In a moment
will fall down like St. Paul in a blinding light
the soul suffers a miraculous change
you become a true inheritor of this altered planet.

I know, I see these men return
wandering like lost sounds in our dirty streets.

This longer version has an autograph note beside the title: 'You may recognise some of the people', and a note to the 'Holbein' reference: 'Can you tell me, is Holbein's signature a skull or some other bone? . . .' KD's list (? Sept. 1943) includes title 'Letter from Cairo'. Pub. *Alamein* 1946, p. xi, with readings from both versions, and with ll. 15–16 (source unknown): 'dry and twisted, elongated like Holbein's bone signature / All this dust and ordure, the stained white town'.

The Trumpet
Hall MS., TS. copy from MS. submitted to *Personal Landscape* (present whereabouts unknown; sold at Sotheby's, 12 Sept. 1961, lot 239), but following punctuation and l. 1 'often' for 'after' from *T.L.S.*, where pub. 26 June 1943, p. 310, with title 'The Regimental Trumpeter Sounding in the Desert' and variants.

Gallantry
BL 53773, f. 54, airgraph to Tambimuttu 1 June 1943. An autograph copy (BL 56357, f. 8) from a letter to Olga Meiersens 2 Apr. 1943 has a note referring to Rupert Brooke (quoted in *KD*, p. 191). Pub. *Poetry (London)*, Sept. 1949, p. 4.

Snakeskin and Stone
BL 53773, f. 98, autograph draft, but following *CP* 1951 l. 17 'mere' (where MS. mutilated); printed here for the first time in stanza form. A four-line opening on f. 98b reads:

> I like a snakeskin or a stone
> a bald head or a public speech
> I hate. I move towards my end
> as a mosquito moves towards her shadow

Pub. *CP* 1951, p. 25 (and see Notes, p. 141), with variants (for which, and conjectural dating, see *KD*, pp. 277, 278).

Words

BL 53773, f. 55, airgraph to Tambimuttu 1 June 1943. An earlier MS. (now lost) has title 'Traps for Words' (see postcard from Blunden to KD 17 May 1943, BL 56356, f. 55). Pub. *Poetry (London)*, Nov.–Dec. 1947, p. 3.

Desert Flowers

BL 53773, f. 56, airgraph to Tambimuttu 1 June 1943. Pub. *Personal Landscape*, vol. II, no. 1 (1943), p. 17, with variant punctuation.

Landscape with Figures 1, 2, and 3

Hall MS., TS. copy as for 'The Trumpet' (see above). An early draft of four lines of 'Landscape with Figures 1' is in a book (Brotherton Collection) given by KD to Olga Meiersens 10 Apr. 1943 (for dating see also *KD*, p. 276). 'Landscape with Figures' is given as three separate poems in KD's list (? Sept. 1943). '1' and '2' pub. *Alamein* 1946, p. vi (in error as sections of 'Desert Flowers'); '3' pub. *CP* 1966, p. 128, as part III of a single poem with the title 'Landscape with Figures'.

Saturday Evening in Jerusalem, Tel Aviv, and Jerusalem

Saturday Evening in Jerusalem: BL 53773, f. 116; one MS. (f. 115b) is a draft set out as prose. Pub. *CP* 1951, p. 132, with variants (listed *S*, pp. 57–8).

Tel Aviv: BL 53773, f. 118, which has an autograph alternative to l. 2 'your indefinite face drawing down my lips'. Pub. *CP* 1951, p. 130, with variants (listed *S*, p. 58), incl. additional stanza (see below). For an early draft see *KD*, p. 195.

Jerusalem: BL 53773, f. 110, stanzas 1–3 only; BL 53773, f. 114, second of two drafts of final stanza, previously attributed in variant form to 'Tel Aviv' (see *S*, p. 57). Pub. *CP* 1951, Notes pp. 147–8, as fragment ending at stanza 4, l. 1 'Now the' (as f. 110).

Apart from two worksheets for 'Tel Aviv' the surviving drafts of these poems appear to have been made in 1944: a draft of 'Jerusalem' includes the words 'I have a beast on my back' (cf. 'Bête Noire'). For biographical material relating 'Tel Aviv' to April 1943, see *KD*, p. 195. Surviving MSS. suggest that 'Jerusalem' was made from the other poems, and this title

155

only is in KD's list (? Sept. 1943), and in a list of proposed illustrations for *Bête Noire* made by KD in 1944 (Brotherton Collection).

FRAGMENT

Version A: BL 53773, f. 121, autograph draft. Pub. 1978 ed.; previously unpub.

Version B: BL 53773, f. 125, the second of two autograph drafts. Pub. *Poetry (London)*, Nov. 1950, p. 7; *CP* 1951 includes earlier drafts (see *S*, p. 58).

Ten incomplete drafts survive, approaching the poem through two basic fields of imagery; the latest draft for each approach is printed here. For the conjectural dating, see *KD*, pp. 198–9.

Enfidaville
EPL MS., TS. airgraph to Tambimuttu Oct. 1943 (date-stamped '15 Oct 1943') with TS. note 'If this differs from the handwritten version sent, please print this version'. Texas MS., probably later than EPL MS. but made at speed, returns to earlier l. 17 'sorrow' for 'pain'; l. 20 'among their'. Pub. *Personal Landscape*, vol. II, no. 2 (? Summer 1944), p. 4, with variants incl. ll. 19–20: 'But they are coming back; they begin to search / like ants among their débris, finding in it'. For KD at Enfidaville, see *KD*, pp. 197–8.

Aristocrats
BL 53773, f. 61, autograph letter to Tambimuttu 11 July 1943 (also an airgraph of same date, EPL MS.). Autograph copy (BL 53773, f. 60) has title 'Sportsmen' and a note at foot:

SPORTSMEN

'I think I am becoming a God.'

The noble horse with courage in his eye,
clean in the bone, looks up at a shellburst:
away fly the images of the shires
but he puts the pipe back in his mouth.

Peter was unfortunately killed by an 88;
it took his leg off; he died in the ambulance.
When I saw him crawling, he said:
It's most unfair, they've shot my foot off.

> How then can I live among this gentle
> obsolescent breed of heroes, and not weep?
> Unicorns, almost. For they are fading into two legends
> in which their stupidity and chivalry are celebrated;
> the fool and the hero will be immortals.
>
> These plains were a cricket pitch
> and in the hills the tremendous drop fences
> brought down some of the runners, who
> under these stones and earth lounge still
> in famous attitudes of unconcern. Listen
> against the bullet cries the simple horn.

'Lt. Col. J. D. Player, killed in Tunisia, Enfidaville, Feb. 1943, left £3000 to the Beaufort hunt, and directed that the incumbent of the living in his gift should be "a man who approves of hunting, shooting, and all manly sports, which are the backbone of the nation."' [Player actually died 24 April 1943.] Pub. *Alamein* 1946, p. viii, with title 'I think I am becoming a God' (the one given in KD's list ? Sept. 1943) and a conflated text, finishing at the penultimate sentence. A MS. draft is reproduced in *KD*, p. 200.

Vergissmeinnicht
Personal Landscape, vol. II, no. 2 (? Summer 1944), p. 3, but with date from 'The Lover', an autograph copy of ? Sept. 1943 (BL 53773, f. 65):

THE LOVER

> Three weeks gone and the combatants gone,
> returning over the nightmare ground
> we found the place again, and found
> the soldier sprawling in the sun.
>
> The frowning barrel of the gun
> overshadows him—as we came on
> that day, he hit my tank with one,
> it was like the entry of a demon.
>
> And smiling in the gunpit spoil
> the soiled picture of his girl
> who has written: Steffi, Vergissmein[n]icht
> in a copybook gothic script.

We see him, almost with content
abased, and seeming to have paid
and mocked at by his own equipment
that's durable when he's decayed.

But she would weep to see today
how on his skin the swart flies move;
the dust upon the paper eye
and the burst stomach like a cave.

For here the lover and killer are mingled
having one body and one heart;
here Death, who had the soldier singled,
has done the lover mortal hurt.

Tunisia 1943

Mein Mund ist stumm, aber mein Aug'es spricht
Und was es sagt ist kurz—Vergissmein[n]icht.

Steffi

A heavily cancelled and variant early autograph copy with title 'A Dead
Gunner' and dated ? Tunisia 1943, on the endpapers of KD's copy of *SP*
1943 (Brotherton Collection) is printed here on pp. xxviii–ix above. KD's
list (? Sept. 1943) has the title '88 Gunner'. Pub. *Alamein* 1946, p. ix, with
title 'Elegy for an 88 Gunner' and readings from both later versions, and
with (source unknown) l. 10 'is a picture', l. 15 'durable' for 'own'.

How to Kill
Alamein 1946, p. vi, source unknown (*CP* 1951 Notes, p. 143, imply a
MS., now lost), but l. 22 'lightness' for 'likeness' from BL 53773, f. 81 an
airgraph to Hall 12 Aug. 1943, where the poem has title 'The Sniper' and
variants: punctuation; l. 4 'into' for 'in'; l. 7 'Now' omitted; stanza 3 reads:

and look, has made a man of dust
of a live man. This sorcery
I do: being damned, I amused
to see the centre of love diffused,
the waves of love travelling into vacancy.
How easy it is to be a ghost.

KD's list (? Sept. 1943) includes title 'How to Kill'. For comment on the numerous MS. draft worksheets, see *KD*, pp. 219–21; a MS. draft is reproduced on p. 221.

This is the Dream
EPL MS., TS. airgraph to Tambimuttu (date-stamped '15 Oct 1943'), with KD's note 'Spacing and punctuation are intentional . . .'. Texas MS. with slight variants (punctuation; l. 13 'the' before 'apathetic'; l. 19 'reach' for 'move') is probably later but less carefully presented; KD notes on it that the poem seems 'just good enough not to scrap, and certainly nothing more can be done with it'. Pub. *CP* 1951, Notes p. 144. Another, possibly earlier, version (EPL MS.), typed, on Italian military letterhead (pub. *Poetry (London)*, June–July 1948, p. 20), attempts a different presentation:

I EXPERIMENT

The shadows of leaves falling like minutes
seascapes discoveries of sea creatures
and voices out of the extreme distance reach us
like conjured sounds Faces cruising like spirits

across the backward glance of the brain
In the bowl of the mind a pot pourri
Such shapes and colours become a lurid
décor to the adventures that are a cycle When

I play dancers choreographers critics role
I see myself dance happiness and pain
(each as illusory as rain)
in silence Silence Break it with the small

isolated tinkle the apathetic buzz buzz
pirouetting into a crescendo B A N G   until
as each scene closes hush the stage is still
Everything is where it was

The finale if it should come is
the moment my love and I meet
our hands move out across a room of strangers
certain they hold the rose of love

Behaviour of Fish in an Egyptian Tea Garden
EPL MS., a TS. airgraph to Tambimuttu dated '15 Sept. 43' but date
stamped '15 Oct 1943'; autograph copy ?1944 (BL 53773 f. 84) has variants:
punctuation; l. 4 'Her red lip'; l. 6 'shell' for 'milky stone'; 'are' for 'white';
l. 14 'sits near her and might coldly see'; l. 25 'But now' for 'Now'. Pub.
Personal Landscape, vol. II, no. 4 (? Summer 1945). p. 2.

ENGLAND 1944

Actors waiting in the wings of Europe
BL 53773, f. 136, unfinished autograph draft on paper bearing deleted
heading 'Bête Noire'; autograph variants include ll. 15–16: '. . . has a
taste / of fairytales or thrillers . . .' Pub. *Poetry (London)*, Nov. 1950, p. 5.

The *Bête Noire* Fragments
BL 53773, autograph drafts: 'A(i)', f. 132; 'A(ii)', f. 133; 'B', f. 134; 'C',
f. 129; 'D', f. 130 (a later worksheet, f. 131, of this approach shows KD
trying to include the rhyme 'princes' with 'lenses'). Pub. *CP* 1951, p. 135;
'B' previously unpub. For the genesis of this poem and the possible order
of composition of its various fragments, see *KD*, pp. 233–6.

Note on Drawing for the Jacket of Bête Noire
BL 53773, f. 135, autograph draft. In a letter to Betty Jesse ? March 1944
(BL 59835) KD commented: 'I'm sending up an excuse (to be used as a
preface) for not writing a poem called Bête Noire.'

To Kristin Yingcheng Olga Milena
BL 53773, f. 128b, autograph draft (the last of several), with alternative
ll. 4–5 'cold Europe, Arab Spain, four finer / poisons for the five senses',
and l. 9 'to the dark plant the juices', added at foot. Pub. *CP* 1951, p. 129
(see *S*, p. 58).

On a Return from Egypt
BL 53773, f. 91, autograph copy 1944, sent, with 'Egyptian Sentry . . .'
and 'L'Autobus', to Tambimuttu ? 14 Apr. 1944 (accompanying letter,
EPL papers). Pub. *Poetry (London)*, no. X (Dec. 1944). For an earlier draft
with additional material, see *KD*, pp. 252–3.

INDEX OF TITLES AND FIRST LINES

including variant titles under which poems have been published

163